Kamala D Harris

Dr. Gopal Sharma

www.diamondbook.in

All rights are reserved. No part of this publication may be reproduced, stored in a retrieval system or transmitted in any form or by any means, electronic, mechanical, photocopying, recording or otherwise, without the prior permission of the copyright holder.

© **Author**

Publisher   : **Diamond Pocket Books (P) Ltd.**
                   X-30, Okhla Industrial Area, Phase-II
                   New Delhi-110020
Phone   : 011-40712200
E-mail   : sales@dpb.in
Website : www.diamondbook.in

Kamala D Harris
By - *Dr. Gopal Sharma*

Preface

Kamala Devi Harris, the Vice President of the US is a great woman whose story is inspiring and begs to be told to give you the will to march forward and courage to succeed in life. As a daughter of an Indian mother and African father, she went on to become a reputed attorney at San Francisco District Attorney's office, ran for Presidency but lost and did so many other things in between, before being Joe Biden's running mate. Kamala's story is one that will motivate anyone!

Are you curious to know more about Kamala Devi Harris, understand how she got to where she is to become the first female, first Asian American and first black US vice president? Do you wish to know her authentic and real story?

Kamala Harris's personal narrative is not just a story of race or ethnicity or gender; it is an Indian story as well. Americans can call it a California story, just like they call Obama's a Hawaiian story. But there is no doubt that her story stands out. It is multilingual, interreligious, and multiracial at the same time. I urge you to keep Kamala D Harris and her words in mind and follow her accordingly:

"*It's time for you, reader, to turn inward and realize the strength that is already within you to change the world for the better.*"

The views and opinions expressed in this book are my own, and the facts are as reported by me and have been verified to the extent possible. The publisher and the author are not in any way liable for the same.

Sources have been referenced and quotes acknowledged to the best of my ability and reach. Any inadvertent omissions brought to our attention and notice in writing will be remedied in future editions.

—**Dr. Gopal Sharma, Professor (English)**
Department of English Language and Literature (DELL)
Arba Minch University, Arba Minch
Ethiopia

Contents

Preface 3
1. The inauguration: A lotus bloomed 7
2. The Girl was me 12
3. I'm speaking 40
4. Identity Matters 56
5. We are the family 77
6. Experiment with the truth 109
7. I am who I am 119
Appendix 135
References 145

1. The Inauguration: A Lotus Bloomed

'Many cultures have naming ceremonies. It is a gift that is an incredible, familial gift. The family gives the child a name and so I come at it from that: not about myself, but for everyone ... Respect the names that people are given and use those names with respect.'

—**Kamala Harris**

I begin the story - in the middle- in medias res. I have to. I begin citing the words spoken by Kamala Harris in her victory speech: "Now is when the real work begins, the necessary work, the good work, the essential work, to unite our country and heal the soul of our nation."

The date was January 20th, 2021. This was the day when a new beginning was made in the US (United States Capitol, Washington, D.C.). The inauguration of Joe Biden as the 46th President of the United States took place on January 20, 2021, marking the commencement of the four-year term of Joe Biden as President and Kamala Harris as Vice President.

Kamala Devi Harris is the 49th Vice President of the United States. She is Ms Harris. She is Harris. She is Kamala Devi. She is Kamala. The name was given by her Indian mother Shyamala. In India, we show intimacy, reverence and friendliness by addressing a person by her first name. In my narration, I will address her as "Kamala" more than Harris, Ms Harris, Kamala Harris etc.

I am going to start narrating the story of Shyamala's daughter Kamala. Kamala Devi Harris who became the Vice President of the US is the central character of my story. Kamala Devi Harris is the name that represents the planet we call the mother earth. She is herself an incarnation of the heavenly. Therefore, I needn't invoke any muse as John Milton did years ago, "Sing, heavenly muse."

What is in a name?

A lot, if it's Kamala Devi Harris.

I am not a versifier. But I got one. Her name is Nikki Grimes. Let me present her verse so that Shakespeare's above cited line could be somewhat balanced.

Life is a story

You write day by day

Kamala's begins with a name

That means "lotus flower"

See how her beautiful smile

Open wide, like petals

Fanning across the water's surface?

They grow deep, deep, deep down

Let me show you.

Now that Kamala Harris, Kamala Devi Harris, is the Vice President of America, you will not ask the question often asked before. Who is she after all?

"Linguistically speaking, we might say, as Amie Thomason argued in her book "Norms and Necessity", a species term fails to refer rather than that it refers to "little robots'."

"How many plausible candidates do the Democrats have now?"

"Three: Joe Biden, Elizabeth Warren, and Kamala Harris."

"Didn't you hear? It's all been an elaborate hoax. There is no Kamala Harris. What people took to be Harris was just a robot designed by Apple!"

The direction we take may depend on our interests- depend on the enduring interests of the language community in employing terms like these. For Indian, Kamala is different, for Americans "Kamala" may not sound the same.

Her name consists of three words: Kamala, Devi, and Harris and all the three words can tell you a story of its own. How you pronounce "Kamala" will reveal who you are. An Indian will pronounce it as "Ka-ma-laa." An American would very comically say something like "Comma-lah." Republican Sen. David Perdue mocked Senator Kamala derisively mispronouncing her name during a campaign rally in Georgia, "Kamala? Kamala? Kamala-mala-mala? I don't know. Whatever." Donald Trump refused to pronounce her name correctly and after the vice-presidential debate, he made fun of her calling her as a "monster." Once upon a time, mispronouncing her first name became a common attack within the Trump camp. When the Fox News host Tucker Carlson wrongly pronounced Ms Harris's name and refused to correct, political consultant Richard very aptly suggested to him, " I think out of respect for someone who is going to be on the national ticket, pronouncing her name right…is kind of a bare minimum." Objecting Senator Perdue's statement Democratic Jon Ossoff tweeted, "Senator Perdue never would have done this to a male colleague. Or a white colleague. And everyone knows it."

Kamala D Harris

Before I move further, let me caution my readers. I am an Indian and I have no issues with her name. I pronounce her name correctly. Indians pronounce her name as it should be. But others find it difficult. Some find it funny. There are full length articles on this topic. Ken Thomas (February 15, 2013) wrote an extensively sturdy article "You Say 'Ka-MiLLA.' I Say 'KUH-ma-la' Both are wrong". On the "Tom Joyner Morning Show", journalist Roland S. Martin opened an interview with Kamala Harris with this query: "Is it 'COMMA-la", or 'KUH-ma-la?' "

"It's 'COMMA-la,'" Ms. Harris replied with a laugh. "Just think of "calm." At least I try to be most of the time."

Kate Woodsome in an opinion piece published in The Washington Post (January 22, 2021) says, "You don't need to like Kamala Harris. But you should say her name properly." It is also added that "not making the effort to say someone's name correctly is a sign of disrespect, when it's done intentionally, it's downright racist."

I have a suggestion to offer. The name "Kamala" has three letters: Ka-ma-la. The first two letters can be safely pronounced as 'come' (unaspirated) and the last one is "laa" as in laugh. Kamala Harris too has this to say in her autobiography-cum-memoir:

"First, my name is pronounced "comma-la" like the punctuation mark. It means "lotus flower," which is a symbol of significance in Indian culture. A lotus grows underwater, its flower rising above the surface while its roots are planted firmly in the river bottom. And second, I want you to know how personal this is for me. This is the story of my family. It is the story of my childhood. It is the story of the life I have built since then. You'll meet my family and my friends, my colleagues and my team. I hope you will cherish them as I do and, through my telling, see that nothing I have ever

accomplished could have been done on my own. (Truths We Hold: An American Journey)"

I have nothing more to say. This is mere inauguration. But I am sure she is not "Komala" (tender), figuratively and etymologically both.

Look at the multicoloured Kolam. It was made for the inauguration by hundreds of artists, citizens and students across India. Many Indians believe Kolam symbolizes positive energy and new beginnings. Several news outlets played on Harris' first name with the headline "America Mein Khila Kamal" (a lotus bloomed in America), and an Indian politician called her VP nomination a "moment of pride for Indians." The festival of Light was celebrated not only in a remote village of Tamil Nadu; it was celebrated in Africa by me. In the US, she was included among so many extraordinary women- Malala Yousafzai, Dolores Hurenta, Ruth Asawa, Serena Williams and Anne Frank in a mural at her *alma mater* Thousand Oaks Elementary School.

Celebrating Kamala Harris as America's first woman Vice President, a unique glass portrait in her honour has been unveiled in front of the historic Lincoln Memorial in Washington DC. It uniquely embodies her glass-shattering achievement. Congratulations!

◻

2. That Girl was me

'I was raised by a mother who said to me all the time, 'Kamala, you may be the first to do many things — make sure you're not the last.'

—**Kamala Harris**

"I was born on Oakland, California, on October 20, 1964. My father, Donald Harris, was a professor of Economics. My Mother, Shyamala was a researcher in breast cancer. Both of my parents had immigrated to the United States. My father was from Jamaica and my mother was from India. My younger sister, Maya, was born in 1967. This is the original Harris family." She said.

"The meeting of the two-my father and my mother- has a bewitching tale to tell. I can tell you my story myself. But I am too busy to narrate it again and again. Let me depute Professor Sharma to retell it making it in the most befitting and interesting manner. I will also not disappear and disappoint you. I promise to you to reappear frequently in the course of the journey."

Meeting together

From India, Miss Shyamala Gopalan came to pursue higher studies in the US. But the life changed when she met Donald Harris who also came with similar goal from another foreign land. They met and fell in love at Berkeley while participating in the civil rights movement.

In the fall of 1962, Donald Harris spoke at a meeting of the *Afro American Association*. It was a students' group at Berkeley whose members would go on to establish the discipline of Black Studies, propose the holiday of *Kwanza*, and help form the Black Panther Party. After his talk, he met a graduate student in nutrition and endocrinology from India at Cal Berkeley who was in the audience. According to Donald Harris, "We talked then, continued to talk at a subsequent meeting, and at another, and another."

How astonishing are the ways of the world! Nay I would say the God. Donald Harris and Shyamala Gopalan belonged to two different worlds. But the fate drew them closer to each other. They were each drawn to Berkeley from two different sides of the planet. They found themselves mentally compatible and thus became part of an intellectual circle that shaped the rest of their lives.

Marriage

Shyamala Gopalan and Donald Harris married in 1963, the year after Jamaica gained her own independence from the United Kingdom. Their wedding announcement in the Kingston Gleaner on November 1, 1963 reported that they were both pursuing their Ph.Ds.

Thank God! Until 1967, it was not legally allowed in at least 16 American states that persons of different races could marry. If California had been one of these states, India's Shyamala and Jamaica's Donald could not have married in 1963. If they didn't marry, the story had not gone so far.

And they both got married in the foreign land. No one from their respective families attended the wedding. We don't know the reason. Even her dear brother couldn't attend as he had just gone off to study in Britain and it was difficult to travel without some extra amount to spare.

Happy Married Life

Let us go back again in time. The time when Shyamala and Donald were together, they rocked literally and figuratively. Amartya Sen who was teaching at Berkeley at the time has this to say about them. "They had a lot of friends and they were growing roots." They led a very happy married life for some time. In fact, they stood out, "with their upper-crust accents and air of intellectual confidence. Mr Harris was "reserved and academic" and Mrs Harris was "warm" and "charming". Anne Williams has this to say about her. "You could tell she was "for the people" quote unquote, even though she had an aura of royalty about her. Here was a woman, deeply brown, and yet she could have flowed from one set to another in terms of race." She was a passionate speaker, fiery and thorough. He was calm and composed.

Kamala: Daughter of Oakland

The year Shyamala received her PhD at age twenty five, the same year Kamala was born. She was born at Oakland, California's Kaiser Hospital on October 20, 1964. It was more than a coincidence that she was born in California and just came to this world a couple of days before Election. It must have been natural that the parents paid more attention to election than to their new-born child.

A copy of her birth certificate shows that she was born at Kaiser Hospital Oakland at 9.28 p.m. 1964. It lists her mother's residence on Regent Street in Berkeley. There was one alteration found in her birth record that many parents can relate to. About two weeks after she was born, her parents filed an "affidavit to correct a record." They changed her middle name from Iyer to Devi. (David Debolt, August 18, 2020).

Kamala is often called the "Daughter of Oakland" as she was born in the East Bay city to two immigrant parents. To a direct response to the "birther movement", her response has always been quick and precise. *Birth place: Kaiser Oakland.*

The MacArthur Boulevard hospital where Donald Harris and Shyamala Gopalan held their daughter for the first time is gone forever. It no longer exists. The building had been taken down as it was too old to sustain.

Kamala's parents had two daughters together. Maya was born about two years after Kamala.

The author of the book *"Berkeley : A city in History"* Wollenberg notes, "In 1964, the year of Kamala's birth, the Free Speech Movement, the first great student protest of that era exploded in Berkeley and helped give birth to the student New Left. When she was one year old, Vietnam Day on the Cal campus began a decade to anti-war activism, and when she was 2, the Black Panther Party started in South Berkeley and North Oakland. By then, Telegraph Avenue had become a major locale of the decade's counter culture."

Little Kamala was the daughter of activism and was looked after during momentous times. Let me give you an illustration.

Fweedom

Donald Harris and Shyamala Gopalan were in the thick of the civil rights movement. Baby Kamala participated in such protests. Kamala Harris narrates one of the incidents in her autobiography:

> *"My parents often brought me in a stroller with them to civil rights marches. I have young memories of a sea of legs moving about, of the energy and shouts and chants. Social justice was a central part of family discussions. My mother would laugh telling a story she loved about the time when I was fussing as a toddler."*

"What do you want?"

She asked, trying to soothe me. "Fweedom!" I yelled back.

Mr Harris and Mrs Shyamala were not just protesters. They were "big thinkers, pushing big ideas, organizing their community." They were not just talking but were ready to fight for their views.

The story how kid Kamala said, "Fweedom" appears in her 2010 book, "Smart on Crime" and also in her autobiographical book "The Truths We Hold: An American Journey." In October 2020, Kamala Harris was interviewed by *Elle* Magazine about her fight for justice. The readers found that Kamala's story about a civil rights protest she attended with her parents as a toddler was very similar to an anecdote from the Reverend Dr. Martin Luther King Jr. In the interview also Kamala Harris said, "My mother tells the story about how I'm fussing and she's like, "Baby, what do you want? What do you need?" And I just looked at her and I said, "Fweedom." MLK's interview in 1965 with Playboy tells the story in a similar way.

"I never will forget a moment in Birmingham when a white policeman accosted a little Negro girl, seven or eight years old, which was walking in a demonstration with her mother. "What doo you want?" the policeman asked her gruffly, and the little girl looked him straight in the eye and answered, "Fee-dom." she couldn't even pronounce it, but she knew. It was beautiful! Many times when I have been in sorely trying situations, the memory of that little one has come into my mind, and has buoyed me."

As a prudent reader, you are already aware of the distinction between happening truth and historical truth. "Happening truth" is the actual events that happen, and is the foundation or time line on which the story is built on. "Story truth" is the moulding or re-shaping of the "happening truth" that allows the story to be believable and enjoyable.

Run! Kamala, Run!

As a child Kamala loved the outdoors. When she was a little girl, her father liked her to run free. He would turn to her mother and say, "Just let her run, Shyamala" and then he'd turn to his daughter and say, "Run, Kamala. As fast as you can, run!"

Kamala would run as fast as her tiny feet could take her. The wind in her face and the feeling that she could do anything made her run as the child artist runs in the film Forrest Gump.

Don't you remember these lines of the film, "Run, Forrest! Run!"

She used to run unmindful of her scraped knees as she knew that her mother was there to apply Band-Aids.

There were merry-making all around. Those early days were "happy and free." The entire family loved music and singing. Her father was her mother's first boy-friend. They were so young and inexperienced. Their harmony didn't last long. Kamala recollected that she knew her parents loved each other very much but it seemed they'd become like oil and water.

Father's Heritage

Mr Harris made it a point to let her daughters experience their father's heritage. He wanted that they should know the father's native land also as they were well aware of their mother's native land. In an article for Jamaica Global Online, He wrote about his daughter experiencing their heritage. In an essay about the Harris family history, on a Web site devoted to the Jamaican Diaspora, Donald Harris writes that he encouraged his children to believe "the sky is the limit," but also told them, as relatives had told him, to "memba whe yu cum fram."

"One of the most vivid and fondest memories I have of that early period with my children is of the visit we made in 1970 to Orange Hill. We trudged through the cow dung and rusted iron gates, up-hill and down-hill, along narrow unkempt paths, to the very end of the family property, all in my eagerness to show to the girls the terrain over which I had wandered daily for hours as a boy."

He continues his essay "Upon reaching the top of a little hill that opened much of that terrain to our full view, Kamala, ever the adventurous and assertive one, suddenly broke from the pack, leaving behind Maya the more cautious one, and took off like a gazelle in *Serengeti*, leaping over rocks and shrubs and fallen branches, in utter joy and unleashed curiosity, to explore that same enticing terrain. I quickly followed her with my trusted Canon Super Eight movie camera to record the moment (in my usual role as cameraman for every occasion). I couldn't help thinking there and then: What a moment of exciting rediscovery being handed over from one generation to another!"

You can also read the article "Reflections of a Jamaican Father" which was written for Jamaica Global Online. Donald Harris wrote, "To this day, I continue to retain the deep social awareness and strong sense of identity which that grassroots Jamaican philosophy fed in me. As a father, I naturally sought to develop the same sensibility in my two daughters; born and bred in America, Kamala was the first in line to have it planted."

In an interview with the *Los Angeles Times*, Kamala Harris recalled visiting her father in Palo Alto after her parents divorced and being told by a neighbourhood child that she was forbidden from playing with Harris and her younger sister Maya because they were Black. While in elementary school she was bussed to an almost entirely white school where she felt like an outsider.

Though Kamala doesn't mention much about her father yet the memories of her trip to Jamaica comes back again and again in her narration. In "Smart on Crime" she writes, "I remember our trips to Jamaica when I was a child. I remember sitting on my grandmother's front porch for hours chewing on sugarcane. My father and uncles would talk to us about the complicated struggles of the people of Jamaica – the history of slavery, colonialism, and immigration."

Mother's Heritage

It's a proud day for many Indians and Africans who have migrated to countries like the US. Many of their children will now see the possibility of reaching the highest echelons of American politics, which wasn't the case even a decade ago. At least some credit for Kamala's rise to such heights does land on the doors of her grandfather and grandmother (maternal and paternal both). Similarly, you cannot discount her father's role and responsibility and due credit should also be given to him. No doubt, mother and motherland both were proud of her achievement.

Shyamala Gopalan gave her daughter the name Kamala. "Kamal" is lotus in Sanskrit and "Kamala" is the deity of wisdom, learning and wealth. It is another name for goddess Lakshmi. It was to help to preserve her identity. The middle name "Devi" translates to "goddess" in Sanskrit. It is another tribute to her religion. "A culture that worships goddesses produces strong women." Mother Shyamala told the Los Angeles Times in 2004.

This was the way to instil in her daughters a sort of genuine pride in their South Asian roots and upbringing. Their Classical Indian names harked back to their cultural heritage. Indian culture was always in the forefront in their thoughts and deeds while nurturing Kamala and Maya. Shyamala was very careful and left no opportunity to make a contact with her parents, brother and sisters in India. Kamala and Maya both still keep their relations intact with them. Ms Kamala Harris still remembers how her mother used to address both of them in her mother tongue. Tamil was her mother's favourite mother tongue and all of her words of affection or frustration came out in Tamil.

Shyamala taught her daughters Kamala and Maya life-lessons that took place during evening gatherings on Thursdays. There the guests included Shirley Chisholm, the New York congresswoman and first Black presidential candidate; jazz singer, musician, and civil rights leader Nina Simone, and poet Maya Angelou. Kamala Harris posted on social media in 2020. "This BlackHistory Month, I want to life up my mother and the community at Rainbow Sign who taught us anything was possible, unburdened by what has been."

Kamala talks about her mother all the time. She often mentions how her mom would bring her along to protests "strapped tightly in my stroller." She has devoted an entire campaign to her mother and credits her for instilling "in my sister, Maya, and me the values that would chart the course of our lives."One of those values was a refusal to be boxed in by societal expectations. Her mother never hewed to other people's notions of where she did and didn't belong, and she was explicit that her daughters should do the same. "If you don't define yourself," she would often tell them, "people will try to define you."

Won't you recollect the phrase from the Queen of Wakanda in the Movie *Black Panther*, "Show them who you are!" I recollect the story of Joe Biden. His mother Catherine Eugenia Finnegan would often tell her kid Joe, "Joey, don't let this define you. Joey, remember who you are. Joey, you do it." In an interview Joe said, "Every time I would walk out, she would reinforce me. I know that sounds silly, but it really matters." Yes, the helping hand and the soothing words matter a lot.

Similarly, she remembers and cherishes those days when they travelled to India every two years. She very enthusiastically mentions her maternal grandfather in her 2009 book "Smart on Crime". "My earliest memories are of walking along the beach with my grandfather and his friends, retired public servants who had spent their careers in government, working to solve public problems. I would watch them play poker and bridge and listen to them talk about politics, corruption and reform. My grandfather would talk to me about the importance of doing the right thing, the just thing. He was part of the movement for India to gain independence, and later became Joint Secretary for the Indian government."

Kamala Harris repeats this claim in her memoir "The Truths We Hold". But the family in India refutes saying there are no records suggesting this. Instead, many of his family members believe he was a diligent civil servant. If he had made any public claim for Indian Independence, it would have got him fired from his government service. It is possible that he might have indirectly supported the movement.

In the late 1960s, the Indian government had sent Kamala's maternal grandfather PV Gopalan to help Zambia manage an influx of refugees from Rhodesia (Zimbabwe). There young Kamala Harris spent time at a house in Lusaka that belonged to her grandfather, one of her favourite people in her world.

That little girl was me

Kamala Harris lived in the building that now houses Berkeley International Montessori School. When she lived there, her family friends Regina and Arthur Shelton ran a preschool out of the bottom unit. They previously lived on Milvia Street also.

Though Kamala had a different and difficult childhood in one sense, she had a rich childhood in another sense of the word. When I say "rich", I mean she had a high value and

Kamala D Harris   *21*

quality childhood. Initially, she was raised by a careful mother and a doting father in a loving home. Her parents were highly educated. They instilled in her the importance of working hard and fighting for the truth and freedom. She attended marches for justice while still in a stroller. She learned that a home is a place not only for shared meal and support but also love in abundance. Her predominantly Black neighbourhood was also supportive and helpful.

Kamala's parents enrolled her in a Montessori school in Berkeley in 1969. And in the fall of 1970, Kamala boarded a bus bound for first grade at Thousand Oaks Elementary. It was 2-3 mile ride from her apartment. In her school what she felt had been told by her half a century later when she got 30 seconds to speak before the senate as a senator, "You know, there was a little girl in California who was part of the second class to integrate her public schools and she was bussed to school every day, and that little girl was me." This line became so famous that the words "THAT LITTLE GIRL WAS ME" became a talk of the town. Her campaign team started selling T-shirts with the image of a girl in pigtails and these words inscribed.

"There was a little girl in California ...And that little girl was me." This thirty second statement pronounced by Kamala Harris became so famous that many thought it wasn't true. The doubt arose as she didn't specify the year. Berkeley Public Schools, Harris's elementary school district, had to release a statement on their official website.

> *"Senator Harris was correct in describing her experience as the second class to be part of the bussing integration program. All Berkeley elementary schools were integrated through an innovative two-way bussing plan, which was implemented voluntarily by our district beginning in 1968. Kamala Harris joined first grade in 1970, which means she*

joined a cohort that had entered kindergarten in the second year of the bussing program, in 1969."

Despite feeling awkward at times like an outsider, Kamala Harris said that she benefitted from this program. That time Kamala Harris was in U.S. She challenged former Vice President Joe Biden on issues like immigration and school bussing. She was praised by many for her performance during the second night of the first Democratic debate then. She shared the anecdote as part of a critique of Biden touting his work with segregating in the 1970s and his refusal to support the Department of Education's plan to support school bussing to help public schools integrate. Biden said that Harris's comments were a "mischaracterization of his positions across the board".

The Tale of Two sisters: Kamala and Maya

Maya was born two years after Kamala. She was born on January 30, 1967 in Champaign Urbana, Illinois. Her full name is Maya Lakshami Harris. Kamala Harris talks about her childhood days and her sister. She says, "My sister was a superhero because she was someone I could count on." Kamala recollects:

"My sister Maya and I did everything together- ballet class, piano lesson, like riding and board games. I knew that if I ever needed her, she'd be there, one half of our dynamic duo. When we felt sad, my mom would throw us an 'unbirthday party.' So we would feel better. Together, we'd eat un-birthday cake, open un-birthday presents, and dance around the living room. Maya was always by my side."

Those days were happy days. Music was everywhere. Kamala's parents lived on well though both were busy in their academic pursuits too. Her father took short-term teaching positions at two different universities in Illinois. Mother settled with her daughters in Oakland and West Berkeley.

Daily Life

Her mother often took Kamala and Maya to her lab, where they helped clean test tubes. When she travelled for work, she sent them to a day-care home away from their house, where the walls were covered with posters of African-American leaders and a young Kamala learned about George Washington Carver before President Washington. She also learned instinctively that she had to follow the way of science. She was taught to formulate her own hypothesis, to use that hypothesis as a starting point for further investigation and to challenge her assumptions.

Close Friends and Neighbours

The family's closest friends and neighbours were African-American. Kamala and Maya attended pre-school and day care at a community centre that imbibed children with Black culture and history. Kamala attended Thousand Oaks Elementary School in the second year of the Berkeley School District's bussing plan for school integration. Kamala and several other black children were transported to the North Berkeley School off Solano Avenue. Kamala Harris still remembers her first grade teacher Mrs. Frances Wilson who was so committed that when she graduated from Hasting College of the Law, she was in the audience. Harris is ever grateful to her. When Kamala had to move to Montreal with her mother and sister, she took with her the sweet memories of her school. Her Berkeley childhood in which she lived in a largely Black community prompted her to attend Howard University. After graduation she returned to the East Bay to work in the Alameda County District Attorney's office.

In an emailed statement Kamala Harris stated, "Thanks to my beloved first-grade teacher Mrs Frances Wilson at Thousand Oaks Elementary School in Berkeley I always had an answer I was anxious to share. Mrs. Wilson had a profound effect on all of us and was deeply committed to her students, a diverse group- ranging from kids growing up in housing projects to the children of people working at the university." Indian sensibility of respecting "guru" can be read here.

Hard to love and live

But the harmony between her parents didn't last long. The breakdown of their harmony was felt by Kamala and Maya both. In "The Truths We Hold" it is described as follows.

"But the harmony between my parents didn't last. In time, things got harder. They stopped being kind to each other. I knew they loved each other very much. But is seemed they'd become like oil and water." Yes, it was hard on both of them. In this world, the divorce is seen as a kind of failure. She must have realized that marrying at will and now going out of it would be difficult to explain."

Her parents separated in 1969, when Donald was teaching at the University of Wisconsin and when Kamala was five and Maya was three. They filed for divorce in January 1972. The final divorce judgement dated July 23, 1973 shows that Shyamala gained physical custody, but Donald was entitled to take the girls on alternating weekends and for sixty days in the summer.

What Donald said about his separation is also noteworthy. In a 2016 essay written by Donald Harris, he discussed the divorce, "it came to an abrupt halt in 1972 after losing a hard fought custody battle in the family court of Oakland, California. But his love for his children remains forever. He writes, "Nevertheless, I persisted, never giving up on my love for my children or reneging on my responsibilities as their father."

Kamala Harris comments as she understands after so many years "had they been a little older, more emotionally mature may be the marriage could have survived. But they were so young. My father was my mother's first boyfriend."

Her mother filed for divorce in 1971. She was so angry that she didn't want to meet him hereafter. She barely interacted with him. Once Kamala invited both of them to her high school graduation, she feared that her mother would not show up. In India, this is also the way to express extreme pangs in love. When you love somebody so dearly and it becomes sour, you taste the bitterness every moment of your life and do not want to talk to the other man about it.

If Kamala's parents' marriage was cause for storm, their divorce was no less so. India has among the lowest rates in the world because of the intense stigma attached around it. Women are blamed even when the reason may be the man himself. Kamala has given some hint about her mother's divorce in her memoir. It suggests that it was a difficult moment for her mother, and a source of family strife. "I think, for my mother, the divorce represented a kind of failure she had never considered," she wrote in her memoir, *The Truths We Hold*. "Her marriage was as much an act of rebellion as an act of love. Explaining it to her parents had been hard enough. Explaining the divorce, I imagine, was harder. I doubt they ever said to her, 'I told you so,' but I think those words echoed in her mind regardless."

By the time they divorced, her mother had already completed her doctorate and was working as a cancer researcher at Berkeley. She retained custody of Kamala and Maya, who saw their father, a Stanford University professor, on weekends and during summers off from school. It is also said that they didn't fight about money. The only thing they fought about was who got the books.

Shyamala and the girls

About a year after Kamala's parents separated, she moved into the top floor of a duplex on Bancroft Way. It was in a part of Berkeley known as the flatlands. They led a modest life, neither rich nor poor. Their neighbours were also common-folk. Mother also helped her daughters in their school projects and cultural activities.

Kamala's mother was a single mother of two daughters. It was hard to live but she lived and educated her daughters as she was educated by her Indian parents. You must have read Barack Obama's stories of his single mom waking him up at 5 a.m. to study, or Bill Clinton's tales of his mother supporting the family after his father died in a car crash. Kamala's early life is also full of vicissitudes and pitfalls. See, how Kamala records her mother's life.

"My mother was extraordinary. My mother was barely five foot one, but I felt like she was six foot two. She was smart and tough and fierce and protective. She was generous, loyal and funny. She had only two goals in her life: to raise her two daughters and to end breast cancer. She pushed us hard and with high expectations as she nurtured us. And all the while, she made Maya and me special; like we could do anything we wanted to if we put in the work."

Kamala's mother was a devoted and sternly caring parent. She volunteered in her daughters' classrooms and would always keep the house stocked with freshly baked cookies. But as a single mother, she had little tolerance for light-heartedness. In the mornings, she'd give her daughters breakfast drinks or Pop-Tarts because, "breakfast was not the time to fuss around." When Kamala and Maya returned home upset from something that had happened at school, she made them reflect on their own culpability, asking, "Well, what did you do?" And she was direct about the challenges her kids would face as biracial children. She didn't talk little-kid talk. She had real conversations with them."

During her formative years in class one (first grade) Kamala started growing among diverse people and children. She could see some professor's children and some from the Black community. They spoke several languages. They belonged to many nationalities. Her home was always filled with children from neighbourhood. Kamala was very eager to cook and bake and she tried her hand to prepare several things though she was too small to do so. She believed that she was capable of doing anything. Cooking and eating were enjoyed the most because it was always accompanied with abundant laughter. She liked a show called "Punch and Judy" where Judy would chase Punch around with a rolling pin. She also liked cookies in a particular shape. "K" for Kamala was that shape.

She was also persuaded by her mother to learn playing Piano. The strict piano teacher would rap her knuckles with a ruler. She would also play chess with Uncle Serman who was a great player. He knew Kamala was just a kid so he would let her win once in a while.

On Sundays, Kamala will go to Church to the 23rd Avenue with the other kids. Kamala and Maya both sang in the children's choir. Her favourite hymn was "Fill My Cup, Lord". Her favourite night was Thursday night. That day they all will visit a pioneering black cultural centre: Rainbow Sign. It was a performance space, cinema, art gallery, dance studio, and much more. It had a big kitchen. Everyone knew them there. They were a unit. That was the reason that they were known as "Shyamala and the girls".

Kamala was very happy with her life. The kind of upbringing she was getting was highly valuable and brimming with activities. But when she was in middle school and about 12 years of age, she had to leave not only the place but also the country.

While mother Shyamala Gopalan was witnessing the birth of a new political culture in the United States, she also made sure her daughters knew the Indian heritage and brought them to meet their grandparents. She also understood that "she was raising two black daughters" and that the US people would view them as Black. She was not promoted as professor when she had been working at UC Berkeley. She was very upset for this and she reacted to it by taking a teaching job at McGill University in Montreal in 1976 and started researching breast cancer at Jewish General Hospital in that city. It was difficult for a single mom of two daughters but she endured. You can imagine, Shyamala moving away with her daughters leaving the sunny California in mid-February to a French-speaking foreign city covered in snow. She tried her level best to make the trip exciting and bought for them their first down-jackets and mittens. They were sad and sullen.

To Canada with compulsion

Kamala and Maya along with mother Shyamala had to go to Canada for work. Kamala was 12 and Maya was about 9. They remember the Mayflower truck coming to bring all their belongings across the continent. Mrs Shyamala Harris had been working at UC Berkeley. She was hopeful of a promotion. Dr Mina Bissell, one of her colleagues, recalls that her friend was promised a promotion that ultimately it went to a man. She bore the hidden scars of discrimination. She was passed over for promotions and dismissed as unintelligent because of her accent and dispensed lessons to her family and graduate students of colour with the same sharp, sassy wit. She was very disheartened and decided to join at McGill University in Montreal in 1976 and researching breast cancer at Jewish General Hospital in that city. "She was a brown woman. She was a woman with a heavy accent. She was a woman who many times, people would overlook her or not take her seriously." Harris said of her in her own presidential campaign.

In February 1976, when Shyamala moved from California to work at McGill University, Kamala was 12 years of age. 1976 is a year when India was under the iron hand of Mrs Indira Gandhi and Emergency was already imposed. In 1976 the Canadian people saw an epic shift in the evolution of the federation. In November, the Sovereignist Parti Quebecois (PQ) came to power for the first time.

Had Shyamala and her daughters arrived a year later, it was probable they would have been ineligible to attend English public school under the provision of Bill 101. Had that been the case, Kamala and her sister likely would have been fluent in French.

Quoi? Quoi? Quoi?

Kamala was enrolled along with her sister Maya in Notre-Dame-des-Neiges, French-speaking schools in Quebec. Though her mother was enthusiastic about her kids learning the language of Molière, Harris said that her time in French school was no walk in the park. At first Kamala and Maya both were disheartened as she writes in her memoir. "I used to joke that I felt like a duck because all day long at our new school I'd be saying, "Quoi? Quoi? Quoi? (What? What? What?)."But that was the beginning when the predominantly French speaking city was distressing and difficult, slowly and surely she saw a lively multicultural world. She connected with students very fast.

Though Kamala thought moving to a French speaking foreign city "was distressing to say the least", it exposed her to a lively multicultural community. She was able to connect with students from different backgrounds. Kamala's relationship with her mother and sister also got solidified in the place where initially no one else spoke their language. Kamala said, "We leaned on each other. We forged a bond that is unbreakable. When I think about it, all of the joyous moments in our lives, all of the challenging moments, all of the moments of transition, we have always been together."

The Big Idea

As soon as they reached there and settled, they started behaving in their usual manner. Life went on as it should have been. Her quest for justice and a taste for power started during her school days. She tells the story of how she and her sister organized a demonstration in front of their apartment building to protest a policy that banned children from playing on the lawn. They won.

This incident of that time is very interesting and has been told a number of times. Kamala was not only dancing and singing; she was also spearheading demonstrations. At 13 years of age, she mobilised the neighboured children to protest against rules that stopped them playing on the lawn in front of their apartment building. In a Children's book *"Kamala and Maya's Big Idea"* written by Maya's daughter you can find how Maya and Kamala got the big idea. What is this idea? Let us read:

"The big idea is to build a playground in the courtyard of their apartment building. The sisters take their idea to the landlord, who very quickly says no. But they're not quite willing to give up. Instead, they start spreading the idea to the other kids in the building. Kamala writes a persuasive letter. Then she starts organizing volunteers. The girls are resourceful and persistent, and they learn that 'maybe' can be turned into "yes" when people see there's a way forward."

This is a true-tale that teaches you how to persevere in the face of disappointment and turn a dream into reality. This is a story in which we see how even children can make a difference and transform their neighbourhood.

FACE or FACES

According to Dunlevy, T'Cha (November 21, 2020) during her school-time in Montreal, Kamala Harris studied for some time at a French primary school. It was called *Norte-Dame-des-Neiges* before moving on the Westmount High School. But there was a school in between. It was called FACE or FACES. It was an alternative public school originally called Fine Arts Core Elementary School and then renamed Fine Arts Core Education. Kamala and Maya both attended the school in 1977-78 (and perhaps for a portion of the previous school year, 1976-77). Kamala was in Grade 8 at that time. In this school she tried out violin, French horn, and kettle drum alongside her studies in history and math. One year, she performed, "Free to be…You and Me" from start to finish.

She had to leave the school as there was no 9th grade in that school. That is why Maya stayed in the FACE at least for a year but Kamala moved to Westmount High.

Westmount High

Kamala attended Westmount High School. I was told by one of my friends who live there that the words "High" and "School" were removed from the building under the signage provisions of Bill 101. To this day, the only word on the building is "Westmount." The school is a very old one and it was founded in 1874. Westmount was previously famous for its best-known graduate Leonard Cohen. (*Leonard* Norman *Cohen* (1934 –2016) was a Canadian singer-songwriter, poet, and novelist. His work explored religion, politics, isolation, depression, sexuality, loss, death and romantic relationships.)

Kamala was a very popular student and her multicultural background allowed her to be a darling of every group. She, according to *The New York Times*, was a "disco-dancing teenage." She was in the arts and was an expert in creating arts and crafts objects. One of her former classmates Trevor Williams told *CTV News* that Harris was a confident teenager with an inclination to advocacy and activism. "When you look back you see certain people who are going to make a big difference in the world-that was Kamala."

Kamala's progressive ideas bloomed at Westmount High too. Let me tell you something more about Kamala Harris. She was in super-six dance troupe. Kamala attended Black community dance parties and found sisterhood in an-all female dance troupe, Super Sis, and later Midnight Magic. I have already told you that *The New York Times* called her a "disco-dancing teenager". You can also witness her dancing-skills in several dance videos available. She was also active and performing in fashion shows, working on the yearbook, and part of the Pep Club whose members yelled and sang at school events. Kamala's high school yearbook entry shows that she was looking forward going back to the US. She described happiness as "making long distance phone calls and her cherished memory entry is, California, Angelo; summer '80." In an entry in her yearbook Kamala encourages her sister, "Be Cool MA YA!" And writes about her greatest source of inspiration: "Sp Thks to: my mother."

As I said, those days Kamala took part in pep rallies. She started a dance troupe "Midnight Magic". Kamala Harris and Wanda Kagan were bosom friends in high school in Montreal. Wanda Kagan described how after she told Kamala her stepfather was molesting her, Ms Shyamala insisted she move in with them for her final year of high school. Kagan said that Shyamala helped her navigate the system to get the support she needed to live independently of her family. Kagan and her experience made Kamala realize the importance of becoming a prosecutor. Later when Kagan told her story to *The New York Times* the readers came to know that it was a special time for them. Kagan was not simply "a person staying in our house now." Kamala realized then. She was welcomed as a member of the family. Wanda Kagan was interviewed by *Mail online* (20 January, 2021) and she said that Kamala Harris's family "changed the trajectory of her life" when they took her in as a teenager. She told how living with the family had a "huge impact and influence on her life, and that Kamala has been "paving the way" for change since she was a teenager.

Kamala was her mama's daughter. Her mother had her own set of values and *sanskars*. Those values persuaded Kamala to change the culture for girls around her. There used to be problems but Kamala used to have solutions too. The girls who had no dates to attend the school prom in a group were invited by Kamala and her friend Wanda also helped her to do so. Forty years ago it was not acceptable to go alone so they decided to change the culture. They started going together.

In September 2020, Kamala posted on Instagram that it was the abuse of her high school friend Wanda that has inspired her to fight for women. "When I was in high school, I learned my best friend was being molested by her father. Once she told me, I said to her, "Well, you have to come and stay with us." And she did.

An incident is still imprinted in her memory and it is worth telling. She invited both of her parents to come to her graduation, even though she knew they wouldn't speak to each other. She wanted both of them there. The father came but when her mother didn't come in time, Kamala was worried. Ultimately she also arrived and she became happy.

During High School, she started thinking about her career choice. Some of her greatest heroes were lawyers. Thurgood Marshall, Charles Hamilton Houston, Constance Baker Motley were her role models. She cared a lot about truth and fairness. She wanted to help the people. She wanted to help the people who were in need. She wanted to be the one people called at the time of distress. She wanted to be one who could help. That was the reason that she chose to go to Thurgood Marshall's alma mater.

"A big part of the reason I wanted to be a prosecutor was to protect people like her friend and change the system." How true it is, if Kamala's family had not returned back to the US, she might instead be Canadian prime minister!

Howard University: This is heaven!

After graduating, she decided to attend Howard University, and not the other big universities. You will be surprised to know that President Joseph Biden and Vice President Kamala Harris both have no Ivy League credentials on their resumes. Harris is the first Vice President with a degree from an HBCU (Historically Black College University). Howard University must have been very proud to see a Howard alumna as the VP of the US. Kamala Harris graduated from Howard University (not a prestigious university such as Harvard or Yale) and then University of California Hastings College of Law.

It is well-known in the US that historically Black Colleges, like Howard University, were founded in order to educate African Americans who were otherwise prohibited from attending college, after slavery.

Howard is a historically Black college. The University had many well-known graduates, including Thurgood Marshall. Marshall was a lawyer who became the first black justice on the US Supreme Court in 1967. He had been one of Kamala's heroes from a young age. College campus with sprawling lawn and brick buildings was on the other side of the country from her hometown of Oakland. She very eloquently remembers walking into Crampon Auditorium for her freshman orientation. She said, "This is heaven!" The time spent there was among the most formative and fruitful of her life. Harris studied political science and economics with the children of civil rights movement leaders Jesse Jackson and Andrew Young. She took every opportunity to connect with her Black identify.

Alpha Kappa Alpha is one of the "Divine Nine" Black Fraternities and Sororities that originated at Historically Black Colleges and Universities (HBCU). Alpha Kappa Alpha (AKA) was founded in 1908 at Howard University, Washington; D.C. At Howard Kamala joined Alpha Kappa Alpha which is the oldest Black sorority in the country, one of the Divine Nine. Here she took part in protests against US investment in Apartheid South Africa. During her freshman year at Howard University, almost every weekend was spent at the Mall protesting apartheid and calling for divestment. One of her friends named Thompkins says "Kamala has an infectious smile and laughter, and just a great disposition, and so it was certainly very easy to become her friend. She was absolutely a pleasant person, a fun person, but at the same time, someone who had goals in mind and who felt that they had a purpose, even if it was just to be the best student representative."

Her first run for office was at Howard University. First, she was elected freshman class representative of the liberal arts student council. It was a tough experience for her as she was new to this kind of campaign asking unfamiliar and strange students to vote for her.

I am sure if anyone challenges her racial identity, he should remember her four years at Howard University. 154 years ago, when this university was founded, Black people couldn't vote. Kamala Harris made it possible that a Howard University graduate of the year 1986 with a political science and economics degree could be the VP of the US.

Kamala Harris has made the influence of Howard University on her known to everyone. On the anniversary of her sorority's founding date, She posted on Instagram, paying homage to her Alpha Kappa Alpha Sorority, and referring to her days at Howard, attending anti-apartheid marches and being part of the debate team: "Howard taught me that while you will often find that you're the only one in the room who looks like you, or who has had the experiences you've had, you must remember: you are never alone. You never have to ask permission to lead."

She chaired the economics society and competed on the debate team. She pledged a sorority. On Fridays, she would go along with her friends in their best clothes around the Yard. On weekends, they went down to the national malls to protest apartheid in South Africa.

In addition to being a student, she had many jobs. She interned at the Federal Trade Commission. She was responsible for "clips" which meant combing all the morning news papers, cutting out any articles that mentioned the agency, and pasting them onto sheets of paper to copy and distribute to senior staff. She also did research in the National Archives.

In the summer of her sophomore year, she got an internship with Senator Alan Crantson of California. Who could have known that after so many years she would be elected to the same senate seat and will be the Vice President of the US?

She once said that she loved going to the Capitol building every day that summer for work but she was even more mesmerized by the Supreme Court building, across the street. She used to go there just to read the words engraved there on marble: Equal Justice under Law. She imagined a world where that might be.

US Hastings

Joe Biden earned his law degree from Syracuse University College of Law in 1968, while Kamala Harris graduated from the University Of California Hastings College of the Law in 1989. Kamala Harris has enjoyed successes throughout her career in law and politics, but this was not one. She failed to pass the bar exam the first time she took it in 1989, according to *The New York Times*. She was admitted to the State Bar of California a year later. She recently said that she consoled a young woman who also failed the bar that "it's not a measure of your capacity."

Kamala Harris went to US Hastings which suited her aspirations and lifelong pursuits for justice. Harris attended the University Of California Hastings College Of Law through its Legal Education Opportunity Program (LEOP). Kamala Harris credits her maternal grandfather PV Gopalan as influencing her decision to enter the legal field. Gandhi, Nehru and Babu Rajendra Prasad in India were all lawyers. Nehru and his father Moti Lal Nehru both were lawyers. Her mother was also in favour of her pursuing a career in law. Kamala Harris also told her law school's publication, "Lawyers have a profound ability and responsibility to be a voice for the vulnerable and the voiceless."

That is why after Howard, she returned home to Oakland. She served as President of the Black Law Students Association (BLSA) during second year. She graduated with a Juris Doctor in 1989 and was admitted to the California Bar in June 1990.

It was 1988, the final year at law school. She used to go to attend the Alameda County Superior Courthouse in Oakland, California. In the process of gaining her first and first-hand experience of the criminal justice system of the US from inside, one day, she got a chance to keep an innocent bystander – a mother of young children – from having to spend a weekend in jail. This incident was a defining movement for her. It taught her how the stakes can be very high even on the margins of the system and that people with limited authority can do justice if they care.

She finished law school in the spring of 1989 and took the bar exam in July. In November the result was announced and to her utter dismay she failed. It was almost too much to bear. Her mother always told her, "Don't do anything half-assed." And she had always taken that to heart. She seemed to be a perfectionist. But she was there with the most "half-assed performance of her life."

She was offered the position of deputy district attorney in 1988 before her final year at law school. Fortunately, she still had a job in the district attorney's office. People would look at her and say, "She's so smart, how could she have not passed." She felt very bad but couldn't do anything. She kept working hard and she was passed on her second attempt. She continued in the DA's office as a clerk till she passed in her second attempt and was sworn in as an officer of the court.

And finally the day came when she rose from her chair at the prosecutor's desk and stepped up to the podium, saying the words every prosecutor speaks: Kamala Harris, for the people.

You, as Indian may ask, why do they say this? This is because in America a crime against any of them is considered a crime against all of them. The prosecutors don't represent the victim; they represent "the people"- society at large.

In both the places i.e. at Howard University and at University Of California's Hastings College of the law, she was more careerist than activist, winning competitive internships and joining academic societies." *The Washington Post* commented.

◻

3. I'm speaking

'Congressman John Lewis, before his passing wrote, "Democracy is not a state." It is an act.' And what he meant was that America's democracy is not guaranteed. It is only as strong as our willingness to fight for it. To guard it and never take it for granted. And protecting our democracy takes struggle. It takes sacrifice. But there is joy in it. And there is progress.

Because we, the people, have the power to build a better future.'

—**Kamala Harris**

After going to Howard and graduating from Hastings Law School, Kamala decided to become a prosecutor. She interned at the Alameda County D.C.'s office and wound up being a prosecutor. Ultimately she became a prosecutor at the San Francisco City Attorney's office. In the opening of her memoir, "The Truths We Hold" she writes that, as a law student, she found her "calling" while interning at the Alameda County District Attorney's Office, in Oakland, California, in 1988. Harris then spent nearly three decades in law enforcement, referring to herself as "top cop." She rose from local prosecutor to district attorney of San

Francisco and then attorney general of California—the first woman and the first Black person in these jobs—until she joined the U.S. Senate, in 2017.

In 1990, after law school post-graduation, she launched her career as a Deputy District Attorney in Alameda County, California. She was appreciated by many and was described as "an able prosecutor on the way up." In 1994, she was appointed to the state Unemployment Insurance Appeals Board and Later to the California Medical Assistance Commission. In 1998, she joined the San Francisco District Attorney's Office, where, among other posts, she led the Career Criminal Unit. In August 2000, she took a job at San Francisco City Hall, working for city attorney Louise Renne. She ran the Family and Children's Services Division representing child abuse and neglect cases.

She tells us a defining moment in her life. She was a summer intern in the Alameda County district attorney's office; she successfully pushed for a judge to return to the bench to release a mother who had been "swept up" as a bystander in a drug dragnet. She feared that a weekend in jail could cost this woman her job, custody of her children, and her standing in the community, her dignity, her liberty.

In the foreword of "Run to Win: Lessons in Leadership for women changing the world" (Schriock, Reynolds: 2020) Kamala Harris tells the story of how she ran for district attorney of San Francisco over 15 years ago. "Running for office isn't glamorous work. I used to go to the grocery stores using my ironing board as a standing desk while asking for people's vote. As people would carry their groceries to their car, I would listen to them. I learned what mattered to them, what kept them up at night, and what kind of America they envisioned. And I didn't stop there; I met and spoke with anyone and everyone that I could and a team of volunteer who became more like family helped me knock on doors and make calls around the clock. On Election Day, I won."

District Attorney of San Francisco (2004-2011)

"There is never a time in the future in which we will work out our salvation. The challenge is in the moment; the time is always now." These words and thoughts by James Baldwin inspired Kamala Harris to take the plunge and try the impossible. "Kamala Harris: Voice for Justice" became the motto. She went to everyone, "Hi! I'm Kamala Harris, I'm running for district attorney, and I hope to have your support." For the voters, even her name was difficult to pronounce and remember. She found that a friend, a pen and a bowl of spaghetti are just more effective than relying on big data and sophisticated voter turnout model.

She was elected District Attorney in 2003, defeating two-term incumbent Terence Hallinan, and won again unopposed for a second term in 2007. Hallinan was considered as progressive as prosecutors could have been back in the early '90s. "The 39-year-old attorney from Oakland unseated an incumbent district attorney, establishing her as a political superstar that would only gather more momentum in the years to follow." Evan Sernoffsky of KTVU said. By defeating him in the 2003 San Francisco district attorney race, she became California's first female African-American district attorney and the nation's first Indian-American district attorney.

Kamala got the guts to run for district attorney because she knew she could do not only the job but also could do it better than others. In 2003-2004, there weren't many district attorneys who looked like her or had her unique background. Such candidates are still hard to find. Even in 2015, a report illustrates, that 95 percent of America's elected prosecutors were white, and 79 percent were white men. Kamala was born tough and smart. Once her mother gave an interview to a Bay Area reporter and she said "My daughter can definitely hang with all these people; she knows which forks to use at the dinner table." In fact Kamala Harris took the words of Shirley Chisholm to heart "If they don't give you a seat at the table, bring a folding chair." She used this as a talisman.

When I read the above statement in the light of her relationship with Willie Brown, I felt uncomfortable. Let me tell you this too. When she first ran for elected office, as a candidate for San Francisco District Attorney, in 2003, she was seen as part of the patronage machine of the majestic, transactional San Francisco mayor Willie Brown, whom she had dated years before; she told *SF Weekly* that Brown was "an albatross hanging around my neck." (She does not mention Brown in her book).

Since her start as a prosecutor in Oakland, Harris has always navigated tricky political terrain, says Jamilah King, a reporter at *Mother Jones* and Bay Area native who has written on Harris's early political career. When Kamala Harris ran for public office in 2003, there was no such thing as a "progressive prosecutor." Kamala Harris decided to be one and defined for herself the job of a progressive prosecutor, "to look after for the overlooked, to speak up for those whose voices aren't being heard, to see and address the causes of crime, not just their consequences, and to shine a light on the inequality and unfairness that lead to injustice. It is to recognize that not everyone needs punishment that what many need, quite plainly, is help."

Back on Track

One of her reputed programs when she was the district attorney of San Francisco was called "Back on Track". "I'm back on tract and I'm not going back." It was a small programme that Kamala Harris started in the San Francisco District Attorney's office. In this programme participants had to plead guilty. It was largely geared towards Gandhi's system of nonviolence. She started "a program that gives first-time drug offenders the chance to earn a high school diploma and find employment."As district attorney of San Francisco, she declined to pursue the death penalty. She's earned the respect of a lot of the people who are doing criminal justice work, who recognize what the confines are. She started a program to provide first-time drug offenders second chances with the opportunity to earn a high school degree and find a job.

Know your Rights

She started holding "know your rights" sessions for vulnerable women all across the city. One of her first actions was to work toward reducing the high homicide rate in San Francisco. She was determined to bring down the rate of incarceration of black, brown, and poor men for nonviolent crimes. Whenever she was in doubt, she kept the words of James Baldwin as a pathfinder, "There is never a time in the future in which we will work out our salvation. The challenge is in the moment; it time is always now." I know that this is a quote I repeat but what to do. It never goes out of mind.

Attorney General of California (2011-2017)

"On Election Night 2010, I lost the race for attorney general. Three weeks later, I won." You will find in this sentence some kind of amazing paradox and oxymoron. On November 12, 2008, after Barack Obama was elected president and Kamala just eleven months into her second term as San Francisco district attorney, she made up her mind and declared her intention to run for California general in 2010. Kamala's biographer Dan Morain, who has been following her political career for long, wrote that day, "She long had focussed on running for attorney general, the state's chief law enforcement officer and a post that can serve as a steppingstone to the governor's office."

On the other hand, at personal level, Kamala's mother was unwell. She and Maya used to take care of her. Shyamala was taking chemo-therapy sessions. Her condition was serious. In a 2018 New York Times op-ed Kamala Harris writes about her mother's condition as follows:

> *"For as long as I could remember, my mother loved to watch the news and read the newspaper. When Maya and I were kids, she'd insist we sit down in front of Walter Cronkite each night before dinner. But suddenly she had no interest. Her mighty brain decided it had had enough.*
>
> *She still had room for us, though. I remember that I have just entered the race for California attorney general and she asked me how it was going.*
>
> *"Mommy, these guys are saying they're going to kick my ass," I told her.*
>
> *She rolled over and looked at me and unveiled the biggest smile. She knew who she'd raised. She knew her fighting spirit was alive and well inside me."*

In November 2010, Kamala was elected state attorney general in California beating Republican Steve Cooley. She was forty six and her rival was sixty three. She promised to bring innovation and reform to the criminal justice system if she was elected. She received 46.1% of the vote, while Cooley got 45.3%. She said, "As one of two daughters who met when they were active in the civil rights movement at UC Berkeley. I am very proud of the work we have done as a state recognizing that, what we do here can change the rest of the country, so goes California. So goes the rest of the country."

Harris became California's first female attorney general as well as minority attorney general as a Black and Indian-American woman. In 2010, voters chose Harris to be the state's 32nd attorney general. In 2011, she was sworn in as Attorney General. She was the first woman and person of colour to hold the prestigious post. "Kamala Harris is a true trailblazer and exemplifies the public spirit of UC Hastings," said David Faigman, UC Hastings Acting Chancellor & Dean. As attorney general, Harris helped get the state's Homeowner Bill of Rights into law in 2013. It gave homeowners who were at-risk of foreclosure some rights.

Kamala Harris has spoken against California's Proposition 8 - which voters passed in 2008 banning same-sex marriages in California. In June 2013, Attorney General Harris says rights of same-sex couples have been denied for a long time. "Each day that passes when any individual is denied their civil liberties and civil rights is a sad day in our country and certainly in our state. And we know that these same sex couples have been denied equal protection under the law for far too long," she said.

As Attorney General, she oversaw the country's second largest Justice Department, only behind the U.S. Department of Justice. She managed a $ 735 million budget and oversaw more than 4,800 attorneys and other employees. As California Attorney General, She fought for families and won a $ 20 billion settlement for California homeowners against big banks that were unfairly foreclosing on homes.

US Senate (2017-2021)

In February 2016, Harris won 78% of the California Democratic Party vote at the party convention, allowing her campaign to receive financial support from the party. In the November 2016 election, she defeated Sanchez, capturing over 60% of the vote, carrying all but four counties. In 2016, she entered the Senate. It was a great achievement then. While 20 African-American women were serving in the House of Representatives, there hasn't been a Black senator since Carol Moseley Braun served one term from 1993 to 1999. Kamala Harris remains ever thankful to California for serving as Senator. The first time she came to work in the United States Senate was as an intern. She was a college sophomore then. She became just the second Black woman in U.S. history to be elected to the U.S. Senate.

She was sworn in on January 3, 2017, by Vice President Joe Biden during his final month in office. She was also appointed to four Senate committees based on her experience. She was assigned to the Intelligence Committee, which held several nationally televised hearings on Russia's efforts to interfere in the presidential election, and how Trump's campaign and the Department of Justice responded to those efforts. The Committee on Intelligence deals with the nation's most sensitive national security and international threats. She also served on the Senate Homeland Security and Government Affairs Committee where she oversees the federal government's response to natural disasters and emergencies.

She also sat on the Judiciary Committee, which oversaw the confirmation of two U.S. Supreme Court justices: Neil Gorsuch and Kavanaugh. On the Senate Judiciary Committee, she held Trump administration officials accountable and was a powerful voice against his judicial nominations.

Following the April 18, 2019, release of the Mueller Report that revealed how Trump and his team expected help form Russia and how he tried to obstruct justice. In a CNN town hall shortly after the report came out, Kamala Harris made it clear that congress has to follow the facts where they lead, even if that means impeachment.

She introduced and co-sponsored legislation to help the middle class, increase the minimum wage to $15, reform case bail, and defended the legal rights of refugees and immigrants. It wasn't so easy to work as a senator during Trump's Presidency.

Kamala Harris noted that the country's most deliberative body was not as it used to be once. When she got an opportunity to make her maiden speech on February 16, 2017 on the floor of the United States Senate, she opened her speech remembering her mother, "I rise today with a sense of gratitude for all those upon whose shoulders we stand. For me, it starts with my mother, Shyamala Harris." She spoke like a lifelong prosecutor and former attorney general of the largest state of the US.

Bid for the White House

In January 2019, Harris launched a bid for the White House. In the first 24 hours after her candidacy announcement, she tied a record set by Bernie Sanders in 2016 for the most donations raised in the day following an announcement. She was initially seen as a serious contender for the Democratic nomination, drawing more than 20,000 people to her kickoff rally in Oakland. In an introductory book published then for the specific purpose Grant Stern wrote, "Senator Kamala Harris is one of the strongest candidates running for president in the 2020 Democratic primary. She has assembled an experienced campaign team and has a mix of grassroots and high-dollar donors. Harris already has a national presence both in person and online that is going to be tough for most other candidates to rival."

Once seen as a leading contender for the Democratic nomination, she ultimately ended her campaign in December after struggling for months to move her low poll numbers. She said in an announcement at the time that financial pressures had led her to end her bid.

She struggled to articulate a clear reason for her candidacy in a crowded field, and her campaign experienced bouts of infighting. On December 3, 2019, she withdrew from seeking the 2020 Democratic nomination. The following lines she wrote, "I'm not a billionaire. I can't fund my own campaign. And as the campaign has gone on, it's become harder and harder to raise the money we need to compete…Let's keep fighting for the America we believe in, an America free of injustice. An America that we know we can be unburdened by what has been." (Medium, October 10, 2020).

In March 2020, she endorsed Joe Biden for president.

Endorsing Joe Biden

Congressman Jim Clyburn, representing South Carolina's Sixth Congressional District tweeted on Feb 27, 2020, "I can think of no one with the integrity, no one more committed to the fundamental principles to make this country what it is than my good friend, my late wife's great friend, Joe Biden. His magnetic words were heard in the entire US, "I know Joe, we know Joe, but most importantly, Joe knows us."

On 8th March, 2020, Kamala Harris tweeted, "Joe has served our country with dignity and we need him now more than ever. I will do everything in my power to help elect him the next President of the United States."

"Kamala — You've spent your whole career fighting for folks who've been written off and left behind — and no small part of that alongside Beau. From our family: thank you," the former Vice President Joe Biden said in a re-tweet of her endorsement.

Kamala Harris had a relationship with the Biden family before the 2020 presidential campaign. She served as California attorney general at the same time that Biden's late son, Beau Biden, was attorney general of Delaware. Joe Biden has publicly and privately encouraged her to stay involved in politics.

"When I started my run for president, I said America needs a president who reflects the decency and dignity of the American people; a president who speaks the truth; and a president who fights for those whose voices are too often overlooked or ignored. I still believe that to this day. That is why I am proud to announce I am endorsing my friend, Vice

President Joe Biden, for President of the United States," Harris said in a statement then.

Running Mate of Joe Biden

On August 11, 2020, Former Vice President Joe Biden, the presumptive Democratic presidential nominee picked Sen. Kamala Harris of California as his running mate. "These aren't normal times," Biden said in an email to supporters Tuesday afternoon, referencing the corona virus pandemic and calls for racial justice. "I need someone working alongside me who is smart, tough, and ready to lead. Kamala is that person." In his note, Biden also referred to Harris's friendship with his late son, Beau. Harris and Beau Biden were state attorneys general at the same time.

An older white man and Washington lifer with deep foreign policy experience was paired with a younger, Black running mate with immigrant roots who had been in the Senate just four years yet still had managed to carve out a national profile. It was a great combination. Besides her professional accomplishments while district attorney of San Francisco, attorney general of California, and senator from California-often the first woman and person of colour in those roles- the two were "raised the same the same way, with the same values."

Biden is 78 years old. He repeatedly referred to himself as a "transitional" candidate. He knew that Kamala was much younger to him. This was a plus point.

Obama offered his congratulations to Harris, saying in a statement that Biden "nailed this decision". "She is more than prepared for the job," Obama said of Harris. "She's spent her career defending our Constitution and fighting for folks who need a fair shake. Her life story is one that I and so many others can see us in: a story that says that no matter where you come from, what you look like, how you worship, or who you love, there's a place for you here. It's a fundamentally American perspective, one that's led us out of the hardest times before. And it's a perspective we can all rally behind round now."

To be true to her, she has a record of fighting to protect women's rights. She's fought for years for reproductive health rights and helped lead the fight for equal pay for women. Who can forget the incident when she questioned Judge Brett Kavanaugh during his Supreme Court confirmation hearings? She flipped the script of the partisan judge and asked him to name a single law governing a man's body. It left Kavanaugh speechless. Trump was surprised. He slammed what he called her "horrible" questioning of his Supreme Court nominee, Brett Kavanaugh. Trump said later, "She was extraordinarily nasty to Kavanaugh, Judge Kavanaugh, and now Justice Kavanaugh. She was nasty to a level that was just a horrible thing the way she was, the way she treated now-Justice Kavanaugh. And I won't forget that soon."

Kamala Harris was a tough challenger and as her grilling of Brett Kavanaugh indicated, she was dauntless when it came to taking on politically powerful men.

I'm speaking

During the debates, she had to underline her statements. She knows pretty well that there are conscious and unconscious biases of women, and women of colour. "Mr Vice President I am speaking. I am speaking," it was Kamala's mild and gentle warning for Mike Pence to stop interrupting her. She was so forceful and her gaze was so much powerful that he had to stop talking. In fact, it was only after the third interruptions from Pence and the additional words by Kamala, "If you don't mind letting me finish, we can have a conversation, okay? Okay." That she was finally able to finish her thought. "I'm speaking" was effective because half of the American population immediately felt a connection to her. Women around the world can easily recall instances when men didn't allow them to speak up. Men interrupt and women join. This is a known phenomenon. Her impact was wide-spread and beyond words. Sen. Kamala Harris won the debate right then and there. Later, she was able to get their votes is a part of electoral- history now.

Elizabeth Hackett tweeted, "this should be 101 taught to all young girls. Nobody taught us this in the 80s."

Harris was the fourth woman on a major party's national ticket. All three women to run for president and vice president have lost: Democratic presidential nominee Hillary Clinton in 2016, Republican vice presidential nominee Sarah Palin in 2008 and Democratic vice presidential nominee Geraldine Ferraro in 1984. The only previous Black candidate on a presidential ticket, Obama, won the White House with Biden as Vice President at his side in 2008.

You may argue that the American vice presidency, as the saying goes, "is not worth a bucket of warm spit." Yet vice presidential candidates, many people believe, can make all the difference in winning or losing – a presidential election. I have pondered over it and came to the conclusion that picking a running mate from a key voting bloc can make a difference. It certainly made a difference when Joe Biden picked an experienced, well-qualified running mate like Kamala Harris. She rose to this occasion and galvanized Americans, who cast more than 75 million votes for her and Biden. This was the most votes earned by any presidential ticket.

Vice President Elect

When I was reading an article written by Kamala Harris and published on her Official Medium account, I stopped at the following lines. I read these lines again and again. I could relate this with my country where farmers are agitating for a long time. Keep in mind 26th January 2021 and read what Kamala Harris wrote on 16th January 2021.

"The violence made clear that we have two systems of justice – one that failed to restrain the rioters on January 6 and another that released tear gas on non-violent demonstrators last summer."

These words were written by Kamala Harris before she became the Vice President of the US. In fact, she has been a prominent advocate of racial-justice legislation after the death of George Floyd. She has also lent strong support for the legalisation of gay marriage, as well as her speeches regarding the importance of the "Black Lives Matter" movement, gained her a massive base of support among Democrats. She's also spoken about reforming the education system to lessen the debt on those seeking a college degree, allowing tax-breaks to middle-class and working families, promoting environmental sustainability, and equal rights for all American citizens. Kamala Harris writes in Medium post. "Together, we will fight for a country with strong public schools in every zip code. A country where one job is enough to pay the bills…" She thanked Americans for their support and called out Black women voters and acknowledged that they made this victory a reality. During her victory speech, she declared, "While I may be the first woman in this office, I will not be the last, because every little girl watching tonight sees that this is a country of possibilities."

Vice President of the US: Inauguration

Following her election as Vice President of the United States, she resigned from her seat on January 18, 2021, prior to taking office on January 20, 2021, and was replaced by California Secretary of State Alex Padilla.

"Even in dark times, we not only dream, we do." This was the key line that told us that history was made on that day. It's the moment more worthy of this book, all the books, all the articles and all the texts written so far. In the celebration, we Indians too participated. We also watched the star studded inauguration. But my eyes were all ears to listen to Kamala Harris. In case you missed it, here is the transcript in full.

Good evening. It is my honour to be here. To stand on the shoulders of those who came before. To speak tonight as your Vice President...

In many ways, this moment embodies our character as a nation. It demonstrates who we are.

Even in dark times, we not only dream, we do. We not only see what has been, we see what can be. We shoot for the moon, and then we plant our flag on it. We are bold, fearless, and ambitious. We are undaunted in our belief that we shall overcome; that we will rise up. This is American aspiration.

In the middle of the civil war, Abraham Lincoln saw a better future and built it with land grant colleges and the transcontinental railroad. In the middle of the civil rights movement, Dr. King fought for racial justice and economic justice.

American Aspiration is what drove the women in this nation, throughout history, to demand equal rights and the authors of the Bill of Rights, to claim freedoms that had rarely been written down before.

A great experiment takes great determination. The will to do the work, and then the wisdom to keep refining, keep tinkering, keep perfecting. The same determination is being realized in America today. I see it in the scientists who are transforming the future. I see it in the parents who are nurturing generations to come, in the innovators and educators, in everyone, everywhere, who is building a better life for themselves, their families, and their communities.

This too, is American aspiration. This is what President Joe Biden has called upon us to summon now. The courage to see beyond crisis. To do what is hard, to do what is good, to unite, to believe in ourselves, believe in our country, believe in what we can do together.

Thank you and May God bless America!

4. Identity Matters

'Years from now, our children and our grandchildren will look up and lock eyes with us. They will ask us where we were when the stakes were so high. They will ask us what it was like. I don't want us to just tell them how we felt. I want us to tell them what we did.'

—**Kamala Harris**

In South India every family has a relative who works in the US. A mother asked her son fervently when she heard the news of Kamala Harris.

"Beta (son) what are you doing these days? Oh, Just a Harvard professor? Not even a mayor yet?"

Not only mothers, even fathers have become more demanding. My elder son Ankur Sharma is in the Netherlands. He is the citizen of the country. I also wish to see my granddaughter or son participating accordingly.

I am narrating Kamala's story through you, readers, to let my great-great-granddaughter know in distant future how her great-great-grandfather felt to witness an India-born woman's daughter to be the Vice President of a powerful country. Let

56   *Kamala D Harris*

her know that this story is not based on a pipe-dream. This is not a story to be told at a binge-party and forgotten. This is a tale of constant struggle and is less romantic than it sounds. Ms Kamala's grandparents, P.V. Gopalan and Rajam Gopalan, foresaw the value of quality education for their children. This Brahmin family from South India 'educated' their generations. They didn't live to see this day but must be overjoyed in heaven. Devi Saraswati must have given a bewitching smile to them and congratulated them on their granddaughter's success.

Can you think of any other country where a first-generation immigrant would go to the highest office? It's a lot of firsts. It is a remarkable time in the US history. We, the Indian middle class, have been watching this event with pride and happiness. Our children who have ever been interested in the annual Spelling Bee contest are now going to be interested in US politics. Young girls in their teens are enthused and elated.

It was said that Biden had picked Harris out of the following choices: Susan Rice, Karen Bass, Elizabeth Warren, Gretchew Whitmer, Tammy Duckworth and Kamala Harris. Joseph Robin Biden was an experienced man. Kamala was chosen among other candidates for the position because she had two distinct advantages: identity-personality and political security. Biden believed that she had the potential to play a winning role for him and improve his social standing. The most notable part of Kamala Harris's choice, in my opinion, has been her personal and personality traits. She has a good articulation and a fighting spirit that has led Democrats to take special account of her. Her taller and angular looks and her body shaking laugh will shake the opponent completely.

Kamala Harris is an inspirational figure to many because of her strong character and characteristics. A lawyer, prosecutor, and former attorney general, Kamala Harris has devoted her to bettering the lives of her constituents while focusing on social issues that help minorities and women. Full of grit and determination, her no-nonsense approach and bi-racial heritage have made her a popular member of the Democratic Party. She has been at the forefront of the US national progressive movements for a long time. Ever since she was elected as attorney general in the state of California she has been in the limelight. Once she joined the US Senate in 2016, her voice became one of the strongest voices. Many find in her the same zeal and fervour as it was in President Obama. She too was an early supporter of Obama. Like Obama, she too has strength and poise. Kamala declares that she wants to stand up for folks who can't stand up for themselves, to serve as a voice of hope and reason in a world filled with lies and despair. She promises to weed out corruption in daily life. Her tag-line has been "For the people".

In today's political landscape, Harris can represent either Black America or Asian America, but not both. "The Democrats are a party of ethnic hierarchies, in which smaller ethnicities—such as Indians—must efface themselves and wait their turn," writes Tunku Varadarajan in *The Wall Street Journal*. But this is only one side of the coin. The other side is: she is the wife of a Jew. The issue of Israel is undoubtedly an integral part of the structure of the political system of the US. She has a close relationship with AIPAC.

Kamala Harris didn't spare even Biden when she ran for presidential elections. She attacked him on anti-racism rhetoric, displayed anti-racist figures, and even rallied in front of the White House with demonstrators. It is believed that she will be able to extinguish the fire of blacks and racists in the United States and show that Biden and his fellow Democrats will not repeat Trump's approach and actions such as Republican policies.

Kamala Harris has a long record of fighting to protect women's rights throughout the US. She's fought for years for reproduction health rights and helped lead the fight for equal pay for women. The proof of her steady and strong track record in this direction is the case in which she questioned the Judge Brett Kavanaugh during his Supreme Court confirmation hearings. She flipped the script on the partisan judge and asked Kavanaugh to name a single law governing a man's body. It left Kavanaugh speechless. During the confirmation hearing, Kamala Harris confronted Kavanaugh about special counsel Robert Mueller's investigation in regards to President Donald Trump. While he could not think of anyone involved in the investigation, Harris followed up with a question about women's reproductive rights. Here is the conversation I heard (Courtesy YouTube).

"Can you think of any laws that give government the power to make decisions about the male body?" she asked.

Kavanaugh froze for several seconds before responding, "I'm happy to answer a more specific question."

"Male versus female," Harris replied.

After a back and forth, Kavanaugh told Harris, "I'm not thinking of any right now, senator."

Though Trump found Kamala "extraordinarily nasty", people around the world found her witty, sharp and adorable. Amanda Litman, co-founder of Run for Something, a progressive group that supports women running for office, called her performance "Olympic level gymnastics of balancing the line of forceful, while not becoming the racist stereotype of an angry black woman. One of the things that makes her particularly different in this regard is she has such a vocal chorus who do not tolerate it, who call it out when they see it, [who] vigorously have her back."

Kamala D Harris

Nisha Chittal opines that "Kamala Harris identity debate shows how America still struggles to talk about multiracial people. Identity is complicated and she shouldn't have to choose just one. Kamala Harris is just one person, and she cannot be all things to all people. She doesn't need to neatly fit into anybody's box. And now, her barrier-breaking vice presidency is also a powerful win for representation of multiracial people in America."

Kamala Harris served relentlessly for a long time. Her performance at all levels had been exemplary. As the district attorney of San Francisco, at the attorney general and as a senator her performance has been more than remarkably good. Indians in America are already there and have been contributing immensely in the making of the US. India born Americans are overjoyed to see Harris marching ahead.

What caused her success? What was the key word? Is there a mantra to recite and succeed? Yes, there is. Kamala Harris revealed it while writing a foreword to the book "Run to win" (2021). She writes:

"If I had listened to what people told me was not possible I wouldn't be where I am today. I wouldn't have had an opportunity to show little girls everywhere that someone like me could win, not only to become district attorney of a major city but to go on to become the first woman attorney general of California and only the second Black woman in history to serve as a US senator and, as of this writing, the first Black and Indian American woman to be on a major party ticket and be elected vice president of the United States of America."

The mantra is: Don't listen to the negativity. Be positive.

Our Prime Minister, Narendra Modi, congratulated Biden and Harris with the words, "Your success is path-breaking, and a matter of immense pride not just for your chittis, but also for all Indian –Americans." I needn't tell my Indian readers that "Chitti" is a common Tamil term for the younger sisters of one's mother, which Harris also used in her acceptance speech of the Democratic nomination for the coveted post.

The Female Barack Obama

In 2015, *The Washington Post* ran a profile of Kamala Harris under the headline: Is Kamala Harris the next Barack Obama? Obama drew the spotlight to her, but for the wrong reasons about her physical appearance. People say that Barack Obama called Kamala Harris, "by far the best-looking attorney general in the country." He wanted to appreciate her beautiful demeanour. His point was that most of the rest of them were old white men. But some listeners found it sexist. I find it innocuous. While Obama apologized for his gender-biased comments shortly after he said them in 2013, his comments underlines the fact how many people view a colour person. Barack Obama himself said this in his book "Dreams From my father: A Story of Race and Inheritance" that he was "a candidate without organizational backing or personal wealth, a black man with a funny name." Brown and Lemi(2021) is right when they comment, "her competence as an attorney general, senator, and later the first woman of colour vice presidential candidate for a major political party will be assessed in part on the basis of her record but also in the context of racialized-gender beauty aesthetics. Like black women political elites who have come before her Harris will have to content with ethno-racial and gendered stereotypes that will largely draw on her appearance and not her political accomplishments. When he found people objecting his innocuous statement, he apologized. "Vice President Harris has already been the "first" many times in her career," says Michelle Obama. "This is a woman who knows what she's doing. It can't be about trying to please everybody or prove to certain people you're good enough for the job. And the vice president wouldn't be where she is today if she let that kind of thing get to her."(Vogue, January 21, 2021)

Barack Hussein Obama and Kamala Devi Harris both share biracial ancestry. He had an extraordinary presidency and she is going to have a notable vice-presidency for the time being.

Dan Morain, a California-based journalist and author of biography "Kamala's Way: An American Life" said that she is an "incredibly talented politician. She is thoughtful, she is deliberate. She thinks more than one step ahead, she thinks steps ahead."

She is tough and demanding: incredibly charming and charismatic. Journalist Gwen Ifill called Kamala "the Female Barack Obama" on the Late Show with David Letterman. In the similar vein Tony Pinto referred to her as "a young, female version of the president" (Obama). She is the first South Asian woman to reach such great heights. Harris and Obama are the only two Black individuals in American history to serve as president or vice-president out of over 90 Americans who have held such high positions in US history. Kamala Harris is the only woman. This is a unique achievement.

Yes, there are similarities between Harris and Obama. Like Obama who is three years older than Harris and who entered politics around the same time, Ms Harris has a similar background. Obama's father was a Kenyan economist who grew up under British colonial rule. Harris's father is a Jamaican American economist and professor emeritus at Stanford University known for applying post-Keynesian ideas to development economics. Obama's mother was a white American. Kamala's mother was an Indian-American. Both had been brought up by their respective mothers when their marriage collapsed. Both are democrats. Both have a background in law. Both have a mixed - race background.

Human mind is such that we tend to compare one with another. But she is not a carbon-copy. She has her own personality and persona. She is the product of her time and circumstances. Her individuality is hers. That is why Obama is "so proud" of her. There are many who find it convenient to 'Obama-size" her and foretell that her vice-presidency will change the life of women of colour in America. But it is not so easy. You know very well that Obama's presidency brought back Trump. Sexism and racism is a fact of American life. But it doesn't mean that her ascent is not worth celebrating. It is "because she made it", as Jemele Hill of The Atlantic says, "to the other side of the barrier."

Her friendship with Barack Obama dates back to his run for Senate in 2004. She was the first notable officeholder to endorse him during his 2008 presidential bid. In the words of Sylvester Monroe, "On that cold January night when Iowan turned out in record numbers for the first caucus in the nation, Kamala Harris was busy knocking on doors, trying to rustle up last-minute voters for Obama (Ebony, March 2008). She's not a fan of being called the "female Obama". When a reporter asked her about carrying on Obama's legacy during her run for president, she said, "I have my own legacy."

Lastly, let me mention that the comparison between them is natural and harmless. Some readers might find it facile and others may call it simplistic. But the comparison has always been newsworthy. Long back in the May 2006 edition of Ebony magazine named Harris and Obama both among the 100+ Most Influential Black Americans. Kamala's photo was number five; Obama's was number sixty-seven. Do you want me to tell you what it means?

Making of History of womankind

I found the book "*The Politics of Appearance for Black Political Elites*" (OUP, 2021) by Nida E. Brown & Danielle Casarez Lemi a unique study. The book is about the everyday politicization of Black women's bodies and its ramifications for politics. The authors opine that after the 2020 election, Black women in the US proved that they were "born for a time such as this". They conclude that the biggest electoral prize of all in 2020 goes to Kamala Harris for her successful candidacy as Vice President as part of the Biden/Harris ticket. This is a historic win. Harris, the second Black woman and first South Indian American senator in the nation's history, was tapped as the Democratic Party's vice presidential nominee after months of anticipation and speculation. This is true. She was able to inspire Americans to cast their votes in favour of her. Biden and Harris got more than 80 million votes. Biden and Harris had gained roughly 51 percent of the popular vote with 80,033,996 ballots, while Trump and Pence held about 47.1 percent with 73,878,907. It was because of the record voter turnout in the 2020 election, prior to which no presidential ticket had received more than 69.4 million votes, the record held by former President Obama during the 2008 presidential election.

This was the most votes earned by any presidential ticket. This feat could be attained as she, along with Joe, could see women's issues, the economy, national security, health care, education, criminal justice reform, climate change and could also address issues such as cyber security(a new front in a new kind of battle)etc. with her sharp negotiating skills, with her poise and calm, mixed with a brilliant understanding of complex national and international issues and laws and an ability to cut through gibberish and nonsense to get to the core of the matter can be some of the features that helped her to win friends and influence people. The middle class voters were hopeful that she was going to do something favourable for them.

One cannot forget what Minnesota Senator Amy Klobuchar said before Ms Harris was sworn in on that historic day, "when she takes oath of office, little girls and boys across the world will know that anything and everything is possible and in the end, that is America." This is worth celebrating and writing. Amanda Gorman, the inauguration poet, was well within her eloquent best when she called herself 'a skinny black girl descended from slaves and raised by a single mother (who) can dream of becoming president." Miss Gorman recited the truths what Ms Harris so painstakingly hold.

In this truth, in this faith we trust.

For while we have our eyes on the future

History has its eyes on us.

Out of our own ...

That is the kind of stuff dreams are made of. From Shakespeare to Carly Simon poets and singers sing eloquently. Even John Keats would have said.

Was it a vision or a waking dream?

Do I wake or sleep?

The most basic tenet of the American Dream: that if you work hard and do right by the world, your kids will be better off than you were. She is free to call herself "American". But she is not only an American. Her life-experience makes her a multi-faceted personality. Kamala has got the Black American experience. She has the South Asian- American experience. She received the immigrant experience. And as an American, she is well-versed in the bewitching power of the American dream. During a debate Kamala said, "There was a little girl in California who was part of the second class to integrate her public schools, and she was bussed to school every day...That little girl was me." The punch-line "That little girl was me" has been a catchphrase since then. Who wouldn't wish to know about that little girl who has become the Vice President?

Democrat of Washington, Ms. Pramila Jayapal, expresses her joy in an op-ed article in The Los Angeles Times indicating her connection with India. "She understands what it means to be the child of immigrants-what it means to be a person of colour seeking justice. There's just so much you don't have to explain to a Vice President Harris and I believe she will fight for many of the issues that are important to our South Asian community."

Nientara, a psychiatry resident at the Yale School of Medicine, doesn't agree with some of Kamala Harris's neoliberal views but tells, "As a brown-skinned South Asian woman who has and is making her professional life in primarily white institutions, it was impossible not to see myself in her. Hearing the names Kamala Devi Harris and Shyamala Gopalan Harris read out loud during a presidential press conference was flat-out thrilling."

Indian businessman Anand Mahindra wrote very aptly on Twitter that there will be an explosion of celebrations by Indian communities claiming her "our own". But we should recognize that Kamala Harris isn't just of Indian descent; she epitomizes what the world should be –borderless and interracial.

The rest is history that took a sweet turn in America. Though an American with a mixed parentage, she is an Indian in many ways. Her mother was an Indian by birth and this is enough for we Indians to celebrate. A well-known and highly respected newspaper of South India "*The Hindu*" carried a catchy headline just a few days before the results, "Kamala Devi Harris and the destiny-changing coconuts from Chennai." The newspaper quoted Kamala Harris phoning her aunt to say, "Chitti (aunt), please pray for me and break coconuts at the temple." What is more to say than what CNN's local partner tweeted that Kamala Harris loves idlis and Sambhar?" She was repeatedly watched when she appeared in an Instagram video with Indian American actor Mindy Kaling where the two were trying to cook Masala

Dosa. Indians were overjoyed and had been sharing the video since then. One could very well note with a cute smile how Kamala was asking her not to call her "aunty" as most of us Indians are taught to. When Kamala says that she has never made a Dosa, women take pity on her.

What more an average Indian wants to celebrate? She is now a household name in India. Her Chennai connection is adding a new twist in the beaming story. Her grandfather P.V. Gopalan was a freedom fighter and lived in Besant Nagar (Madras, now Chennai). Kamala got her first lessons in civil rights activism while going for long walks with her grandfather."My grandfather would talk to me about the importance of applying an unflinching ethical lens to every single problem you face." Kamala Harris stated in an interview. In another interview with Aziz Haniffa Kamala Harris said that she was very proud of her Indian roots.

"I am proud to be who I am, I am proud of the influences that my family have had on my life, and similarly the influence of my mentors and colleagues and friends. One is not to the exclusion of the other- I believe that point is at the heart of this matter. We have to stop seeing issues and people through a plate-glass window as though we were one-dimensional. Instead, we have to see that most people exist through a prism and they are a sum of many factors-everyone is that way, and that is just the reality of it."

For Indians "family" is the key. We treat the entire world as a family. This makes us familiar. Familiarity is our heart and soul. If a foreigner looks at our words for relations and relatives, she will be surprised. For an American there are just two words- "uncle" and "aunt". We have a dozen. Ms Harris is a respectable name but for Indians this is not the right and respectable way to address a daughter of the family. She is "Kamala" and her sister is "Maya".

Optimism and problem solving are part of her DNA. According to her biographer "that little girl grew up to be a tough, sharp-witted, exacting, hardworking, smart, multilayered, and multicultural woman. Kamala Harris misses little and forgets even less. She is a foodie who finds joy in cooking and dining at the fine restaurants and out-of –the –way joints. Mostly, she is her mother's daughter." She is so worried about everything that once she proclaimed, "Let me just tell you, I was born worrying. I had a mother who was always worried; I had a grandmother who was worried. It's kind of in my blood." Here worry and care are the two sides of the same coin.

"You didn't have to be confined by anyone else's idea of what it means to be black. You could be a fine arts student and also be class president. You could be homecoming queen and be the head of the science club. You could be a member of a society and be in student government and want to go to law school, and it encouraged you to be your full self." She told CCN's Dana Bash on "state of the Union" in September 2020.

She realized that she had a keen sense of argumentation. Code switching is embedded in Indians' DNA. It's not style, it's a survival tool. Her cultural adeptness makes her an intelligent politician. She was seen jamming to a drumline and making dosas with Mindy Kaling and also dragging Joe Biden for his record on school desegregation. Compromise and consensus are her key personality traits. She uses these traits to bring people together. She is a barrier breaking figure as Kamala Harris is a woman of colour – Black woman. Mothers in the black community tell their sons and daughters, "You have to work twice as hard to get half as much." Kamala wrote:

> "*Years from now, our children and our grandchildren will look up and lock eyes with us. They will ask us where we were when the stakes were so high. They will ask us what was like. I don't want us to just tell them how we felt. I want us to tell them what we did.*"

God had something a little extra for her, I suppose. Brazile, the first woman to run a major presidential campaign, is right when she says that Kamala Harris will have to show millions of Americans, not just how she leads but how women of colour across all industries can lead. The country will have to adjust to the fact that it's supposed to look different.

Daughter

Much has been written about Kamala Harris as a daughter. She leaves no opportunity to tell the world how amazing her mother is to her. She says, "My mother pushed us hard and with high expectations as she nurtured us. And all the while, she made Maya and mee feel special like we could do anything we wanted to if we put in the work."

She is not only grateful to her mother, she is also thankful to her as she was a good parent. "From my grandparents, my mother learned that it was service to others that gave life purpose and meaning. And from my mother, Maya, and I learned the same."

Kamala learned from her mother the value and belief in the dignity of work. Ms Shyamala, her mother taught her through her words and actions that no matter how you earn a living, whether you're a caregiver or truck driver, grocery store clerk or small business owner, every job has inherent value and worth.

Kamala's love for her mother is so deep-rooted that it is reflected in her love for her children. Though she is not the biological mother of her son and daughter, she considers them as her own children. She is clear about it and says.

"Nothing makes a child feel more secure than being tucked in by a parent at the end of the day. Getting a kiss and a hug, a good night story, falling asleep to the sound of their voice... Nothing is more important to a person than talking with tethering child at night before the child goes to sleep,

answering their questions, comforting and reassuring them in the face of any fears, making sure they know that everything will be okay. Parents and children everywhere relate to these rituals. They are part of the human experience."

Mother

Kamala Harris once made a speech. In her speech, she not only touched on the importance of family but went into detail on how she defines her own. "Family is my husband, Doug, who I met on a blind date set up by my best friend." she said. "Family is our beautiful children, Cole and Ella, who call me 'Momala'." What is Momala? Do you know? Momala is an alternative for 'stepmom'.

In a 2019 *Elle.com* essay, Kamala Harris shared the personal details how and when she met her husband. Doug Emhoff was a divorced dad with two kids named Cole and Ella.

"I was determined not to insert myself in their lives until Doug and I had established we were in this for the long haul. Children need consistency; I didn't want to insert myself into their lives as a temporary fixture because I didn't want to disappoint them. There's nothing worse than disappointing a child."

A Jewish parenting site *Kveller.com* points out, "Momala" isn't just a play on Kamala's name. Emhoff and his kids are Jewish, and "mamaleh" is a Yiddish word that means "little mama" (but is often used as a term of endearment for kids). Now, it's unclear if Cole and Ella made the explicit connection between the endearing nickname and the Yiddish word "mamaleh".

Friend

If I don't include Ms Kagan's name and tell you about her story and also don't tell you about her friendship with Kamala Harris, I will not be able to do justice with both of them. In fact, it was Kagan who first told her part of story publicly to the *New York*

Times and didn't mince or hide words. She told that living with Kamala's family in her high school days in Montreal was an experience of a life-time. She had never had good food like that. She was given Indian delicious food with Shyamala's motherly love and soul-soothing counselling.

Kamala Harris spent her adolescent years in Canada. She studied at Westmount High. She was an extrovert American girl who dreamt of becoming a lawyer and liked dancing to Diana Ross and Michael Jackson. There she met Wanda Kagan. Kamala and Wanda used to attend Black community dance parties and found sisterhood in all-female dance troupe, super six, Later Midnight Magic. They were also active; performing in fashion shows, working on the yearbook and part of the Pep Club whose members yelled and sang at school events.

They became friends because both were biracial. Wanda's father was Black and mother was White Jewish. Kamala's father was Jamaican and mother was an Indian. The two girls became friends.

The noble character of Kamala and her mother Shyamala shouldn't be left without presenting in detail. When they came to know that Wanda was being abused by her stepfather, they asked her to come and join them. You will be surprised to know that Kagan's stepfather was molesting her. Kagan confided in her friend her secret. This experience made Kamala's determination stronger in protecting women and children.

How could they not help her friend in distress? They had been given Indian sanskaras by their parents. Ultimately, that difficult period was over. Kamala was so much moved with all this that she decided to be a prosecutor. Ms Kagan was also so much moved staying with Maya and her mother. They just treated her like family. They indirectly taught her certain human values that she is still following. The name of Wanda Kagan's daughter is Maya. You can understand that both the friends are bosom friends. She still remembers her as a teenager,

> *"Her smile, her laugh, the way she would go into a crowd during the campaign and giggle with kids- that are who she is. That's the raw Kamala."*

Wanda Kagan is presently Administrative Agent in the Academic Affairs Directorate of CIUSS West-Central Montreal. In her high school, Kamala Harris was not only fighting for her friend's rights and dignity, she was preparing herself for doing the same for the entire humanity.

Tit Bit about Kamala Harris

I found it hard to get some personal tit-bits about Kamala Harris. Perhaps she shared few personal details.

At home, Kamala Harris is surrounded with lawyers. Her husband Doug is a lawyer. Sister Maya's husband Tony is a lawyer. Maya's daughter Meena's a lawyer too. There will always be questions, tough and direct. Oh my Gosh!

Her most fervent online supporters were called the "KHive phrase inspired by Beyoncé's loyal group of fans, the "Beyhive". #KHive is the hashtag used by an informal online community supporting Kamala Harris, the 49th Vice President of the United States. The term KHive, pronounced K-Hive, also refers to that online community. It is not formally affiliated with the campaign. Ms Harris joined Mr Biden's team as a political star. Though her own presidential bid failed to find its focus and sputtered to an early halt, it earned her a devoted fan following (they call themselves the #KHive).

Foodie and Great Cook

She is a foodie. She finds joy in cooking. She's an enthusiastic cook who bookmarks recipes from the New York Times' cooking section and has tried almost all the recipes from Alice Waters' The Art of Simple Food. Her go-to dinner entree is a simple roast chicken. Haven't you seen her preparing masala dosa? She likes dining at fine restaurants and out of the way joints. She has listed Idli with a "really good Sambhar" and "any kind of tikka" as her favourite Indian dishes. Many housewives in India immediately got connected with her when they saw Kamala talking with Mindy Kaling about storing spices in recycled coffee jars. A photo of a young Harris wearing a sari along with her comments about her late Tamil grandmother has been a constant source of discussion between my wife Shashi and my daughter in law Akshitara.

Book Lover

Whatever you say Kamala Harris is the daughter of academics. She will forever be their daughter. She's excited by experiments, such as The Mayor of Stockton's plan for a form of universal basic income which gets a big shout-out in her memoir The Truths We Hold. Even her 2009 book Smart on Crime where you come across a barrage of data first, you find Kamala Harris trying to find like a "cringingly trendy professor" when "she calls on readers to rock the crime pyramid!" says Cris Taylor eloquently. Perhaps she understood from her early days when she used to visit Rainbow Sign and was in the company of James Baldwin, Shirley Chisholm, Alice Walker, Maya Angelou and Nina Simone that "there is no better way to feed someone's brain than by bringing together food, poetry, politics, music, dance and art." When she started in the D.A.'s office, she recounts, she described herself as "a hard worker, A perfectionist. Some who didn't take things for granted." These statements spring from erudite wisdom and are got from extensive reading.

Kamala is a book lover. She inherited it from her parents. "When they (Kamala's parents) divorced, they didn't fight about money. The only thing they fought about was who got the books." Her favourite books include Native Son by Richard Wright, The Kite Runner by Khaled Hosseini, The Joy Luck Club by Amy Tan, Song of Solomon by Toni Morrison, and The Lion, the Witch and the Wardrobe by C.S. Lewis. Books helped her to develop empathy for others.

Fitness First

She typically wakes up around 6 a.m. and works out for half an hour on the elliptical or SoulCycle. She likes to lift weight. Back in September 2020, during a conversation with former US President Barack Obama which was published on Twitter, Kamala Harris had told, "I work out every morning, regardless of how much sleep I've had. It's just the best way to start the day." It's also reported that Emhoff and Kamala both are of the same age, also like taking six or seven miles walks together. She'll start the day with a bowl of Raisin Bran with almond milk and tea with honey and lemon before leaving for work. According to one researcher (Nyugen, H. 2020, and Sept 22. Kamala Harris: Daily routine. *Balance the Grind*) her daily routine has been as follows:

- 6:00 AM- Morning Spin Class
- 6:30 AM- Breakfast Time
- 8:00 AM- Call Colleagues on Way to Work
- 9:00 AM- Travel for Work
- 12:00 PM- Eat Lunch
- 1:00 PM- Work, Campaign, and Attend Meetings
- 6:00 PM- Read Cookbook
- 7:00 PM- Family Dinner
- 8:00 PM- Hot Bath
- 9:00 PM- Drink Chamomile Tea
- 11:00 PM- Unwind
- 12:00 AM- Sleep

As a family woman, a working woman and now the Vice President of the United States of America, it's an understatement that Vice President Harris has a lot on her plate. She understands, more than most people, that we only have 24 hours in a day to maximize our time. She prioritizes her health and fitness, along with her goals and family time. On a typical day, Vice President Harris wakes up at 6 am and tries to work out every morning. She enjoys cycling, either participating in solo cycling or joining a SoulCycle class. Harris makes sure to prioritize working out, because health and wellness are important to her (Nguyen, 2020).

Awards and Honours

In 2005, the National Black Prosecutors Association awarded Kamala Harris the Thurgood Marshall Award. That year, she was featured along with 19 other women in a Newsweek report profiling "20 of America's Most Powerful Women". A 2008 New York Times article published later that year also identified her as a woman with potential to become president of the United States, highlighting her reputation as a "tough fighter". In 2013, Time named Harris as one of the "100 Most Influential People in the World". In 2016, the 20/20 Bipartisan Justice Centre awarded Harris the Bipartisan Justice Award along with Senator Tim Scott. Biden and Harris were jointly named Time Person of the Year for 2020. "And America bought what they were selling: after the highest (voter) turn out in a century. They racked up 81 million votes and counting, the most in presidential history, topping Trump by some 7 million votes and flipping five battleground states" Time wrote.

Kamala Harris will forever be first. This 'firstness' will ever be celebrated by the world that values forerunners. People celebrate first because they are historic. People take them as role-models. Perhaps because of this, Kamala Harris announced in her acceptance speech, "While I may be the first woman in this office, I will not be the last. The generations of Black women, Asian, white, Latina, Native American women who throughout our nation's history paved the way for this moment."

Kamala Harris embodies progress. Once, she closed out her speech to the music of Mary J. Blige's Work. Now, I close this chapter with the same lines in verse.

There's so many-a girls

I hear you been running

From the beautiful queen

That you could be becoming …

Read the book of my life

And see I've overcome it.

◻

5. We are the Family

'Family means everything to me. I've had many titles throughout my career, but Momala will always be the one that means the most to me.'

—**Kamala Harris**

Who knows better than us about "family"? Even in the US, family has been a foundation of American values. In 1778 John Adams firmly believed that "the foundations of national morality must be laid in private families." Historian Nancy F. Cott says that one of the few things most people can agree upon in the US is family-values. In her book "Public Vows", *Nancy* demonstrates that marriage is as important as it helps shape the future of *family* life and the impact of marriage law is great on the American social *structure*.

Kamala Harris has been in politics for nearly a decade, she's become a household name now. Everyone wants to know her personal background and the policies she's passionate about, to her inspiring parents, grandparents, and equally talented sister and niece. We want to know it all. Her love-story and marriage at the age of 50 is also not an ordinary life-event. Kamala herself didn't have children before marrying Emhoff, but after they met she became a stepmom to his two kids, Cole and Ella. Didn't you spot both the children by her side during the inauguration?

Kamala Harris, the daughter of Indian and Jamaican immigrants, was raised with both Christian and Hindu practices, while her husband, who is white, grew up attending Jewish summer camp. (At their wedding, she took part in the Jewish ritual of smashing a glass.) All this sounds interesting and should invariably be part of this book on her. She accepts this when she says, "I was raised that you don't talk about yourself. But I've also realized that in order to form the relationships, it's important to let people know about the people." Kamala's family believes that she is always being there for all of them: the kids, the little nieces and her sister and elderly people. She has the knack of bringing other people along with her.

Kamala Harris says that family is not only blood but "the family you choose". She has a very large family in this way. For instance, Chrisette Hudlin is also a member of her family. It was during her wedding she announced her bid for attorney general and to whose children she is godmother. It was Hudlin who introduced her to the "funny, self-deprecating" entertainment lawyer who would become her husband.

This chapter is marked to tell you everything you wish to know about her immediate family and her extended one as well. As Indians, if you know about her Indian background also, it will add to your knowledge and understanding. Her mother taught her that food is family and family is love. Kamala's sister Maya was a trustworthy sister in weal and woe. Their father encouraged Kamala to be strong and brave. Their grandparents from India taught them India's cherished values and culture. Their visits to India and Jamaica broadened their mind. Kamala's friends at school were bosom friends. They were always ready to help. As a student, Kamala had fun and frolic. Her teachers were inspiring and great. Many close friends and relatives broadened her outlook. Her life-experience is unique. She found role models around her. The result is her adorable personality.

Whenever she gives credit to others too her mother and family comes first. Once she said that along with so many lessons she's absorbed along the way – foundational wisdom from her mother; encouragement and guidance from family members, friends and trusted mentors; and the powerful examples she has witnessed, both good and bad, that has shaped her understanding of what it takes to lead effectively, what it takes to achieve one's objectives, and what we owe to one another in the process. These lessons have been informed by her life experiences and leavened by their application over the course of her career.

Jeffrey Gentleman and Suhasini Raj (The New York Times: August 16, 2020) underscores how Kamala Harris's family in India helped shape her values. Kamala Devi Harris gained part of her foundation from mother's side of the family which defied stereotypes in India and promoted equality for women. Kamala Devi Harris is the part of a family, a joint family. In this family, there are her mother, sister, husband, children and so many relatives. In the large family, the entire black community, nay, the entire US included. As a daughter of an Indian immigrant and an African father, she is there to make sure that the families around who see the American dream for their children are not left behind. They should be helped to realize their dreams. Kamala is free and fearless as her mother and is ready to speak her mind freely and fearlessly.

Kamala is not worried about failings and falling. She tells everyone, "What defines us is how well we rise after falling." She remembers how she failed as a student and how she has to abandon her plans to run for President. She is of the view, "One day, I'm going to have that job."

Kamala Harris gives the credit of her success to her family. In her family, her mother comes before the others. Every time she mentions her mother she becomes emotional and it becomes difficult for her to maintain her composure. We have a separate chapter on her mother and it is worthwhile to introduce to you some other members of her family. It is important to underscore their value in making her what she is now and what she will be in future. In the preface of her memoirs she very aptly concludes underscoring the family.

"I want you to know how personal this is for me. This is the story of my family. It is the story of my childhood. It is the story of the life I have built since then. You'll meet my family and my friends, my colleagues and my team. I hope you will cherish them as I do and, through my telling, see that nothing I have ever accomplished could have been done on my own."

Ancestral Village

Let me start her story from the beginning. The story doesn't start in the haze of antiquity. It starts sometime in the early twentieth century. Thulasendrapuram or Thulasendirapuram is a village in Tiruvarur District, Tamil Nadu (India). It is about 7 km from Manargudi and 35 km from Tiruvarur. In 2020, its population was just about 350. The maternal grandfather of Kamala Devi Harris was born there in 1911.

Maternal Grand Father

Painganadu Venkataraman Gopalan was born into a Tamil Brahmin family in 1911 in Thulasenthirapuram, Mannargudi, a village in the erstwhile Tanjore District, Madras Presidency, in India. This district is very famous for Karmkandi erudite Brahmins, the main group from which Hindu Brahmin priests hail. Mr Gopalan's forefathers were also pious Brahmins. Like many traditional Brahmins, he was also a devotee of goddess

Saraswati, the goddess of learning. Raghava Krishnaswami Raghavan, a former CBI Director and until last year India's High Commissioner to Cyprus narrated Gopalan's story on News18 dated August 17, 2020 as follows:

"P.V. Gopalan was an intelligent and ambitious young man. He was educated so he decided to reach out beyond Madras for livelihood. The British rulers wanted English speaking clerks in North Indian capital city. Delhi gave him a government job of an assistant. "The central government in Delhi was always warm towards young graduates, especially those from the South, because 'Madrasis', as people from this region were generally known, were regarded as mild, obedient and loyal, with a solid knowledge of English, the official language. It was his venturesomeness that persuaded Gopalan to go to distant Delhi, a two nights' train journey from Madras (now Chennai) by the fabled Grand Trunk Express."

Raghvan continues, "Like all typical South Indian bureaucrats, he had no distraction but concentrated on his job, earning some money and a reputation…" He was not a proverbial 'frog in the well but was great enterprising to go to a troubled continent such as Africa, and did not wilt under the local harsh conditions of living.' Before retirement he got a chance to work in Zambia. He was sent on a diplomatic mission by India to assist the African nation when it gained independence. After retirement he settled in Madras. These are the parts of the story.

He knew the value of education, quality education. That is why he never missed an opportunity to tell his son and daughters to study well. You can very well imagine that he wanted to see his children trying their luck even beyond the length and breadth of newly Independent India. India became free in 1947. That was the time when Nehru brought socialism and hope even for the downtrodden and weak. Mr Gopalan was not a poor man. He was able to educate his children well.

Kamala Harris tells less about her paternal grand-father but when it comes to her maternal grandfather, she is all praise for him. When she shares her childhood memories, she becomes very eloquent talking about walking down the beach hand in hand with her Indian grandfather Mr P.V. Gopalan. He was a thorough gentleman. He never raved about the great things that he had done in Delhi and elsewhere. He was down-to-earth and self-satisfied family man.

In terms of India's caste system, the family was at the top. They were Tamil Brahmins. But he never looked down at the lower castes and valued quality education. He left the village as a young man to take a job as a stenographer for the British colonial government. Kamala Devi wrote in her memoir that he had been part of India's independence movement. After independence in 1947, he continued as a civil servant for the new Indian government.

When she was a child, every two or three years they travelled to India to visit her grandparents along with her mother and younger sister. Her earliest memories are of walking along the beach with her grandfather and his friends-retired public servants who had spent their careers trying to make India a better place. Mr Gopalan would talk to his granddaughter about the importance of applying an unflinching ethical lens to every single problem we face. He defied the conservative stereotypes of his era, embodying a progressive outlook on public service and unwavering support for women, especially in terms of their education, that was years ahead of his time. He was Joint Secretary for the Indian Government, a post similar to the US Deputy Secretary of State, and he had a number of fascinating assignments, including several years as an advisor to the government of Zambia in Africa. "I remember the stories that they would tell and the passion with which they spoke about the importance of democracy," Ms. Kamala Harris said in a 2018 speech to an India- American group. "As I reflect on those moments in my life that have had the most impact on who I am today — I wasn't conscious of it at the time — but it was those walks on the beach with my grandfather in Besant Nagar that had a profound impact on who I am today."

"Los Angeles Times" published after interviewing Balachandran and his daughter something you would love to read. It will make you smile too.

"In photos, Gopalan stares gravely from behind oversized glasses, but with his granddaughters he cracked sly jokes. When Rajam left the house, Gopalan, a strict vegetarian who avoided even eggs, sometimes cast Harris and her sister a conspiratorial look and said: "OK, let's have French toast.

He taught Harris to play five-card stud poker. If she misbehaved, Gopalan would take her into another room and pretend to slap her on the hand — urging her to shriek in mock pain — before re-emerging to tell Shyamala, "I handled it".

During 1991, Kamala Harris and her family went to Chennai. It was a very important occasion when the whole family gathered to celebrate P.V. Gopalan's 80th birthday. His wife Mrs Rajam was also there. Their great granddaughter Meena was also present. Four generations were under one roof were present. That was the day Mr Gopalan must have been very proud of his life well-spent.

"The Truths We hold", Kamala's memoir, has much to say about Mr Gopalan: P.V. Gopalan had been part of the movement to win India's independence. He used to joke that her activism would get him in trouble one day. But he knew that was never going to stop her.

Maternal Grandmother

Mr Gopalan was married to Rajam Gopalan. Rajam was betrothed to him at age twelve and began living with him at sixteen. She was quite a force in her own right. "The Truths We Hold" has this to say about Rajam Gopalan: She had never attended high school but she was a skilled community organizer. She would take in women who were being abused by their husbands, and then she's call the husbands and tell them they'd better shape up or she would take care of them. She used to gather village women together, educating them about contraception. Mr Gopalan used to be happy to see his wife but showed as if he was a worried husband. He would often joke that her community activism would be the end of his career. But Rajam remained as she was. She remained vibrant and interested in the worldly affair throughout her life.

Mrs Rajam had to keep her motherly love for her four children under wraps. She was soft on stray animals but strict about throwing waste outside. It was her constant vigil that kept her children vigilant and sharp. She was lucky that her son and daughters were studious and busy in their work. But when they got into some mischief, she used to be careful. Balu and Shyamala were two years apart in age and whenever they used to play childlike pranks and hide under beds, Rajam used to bring them out using the handle of a domestic broom.

She was also very strict about certain human values. She wanted her husband should remain unblemished and pure. She didn't allow strangers to enter home as she wanted no one to come there to offer her husband any bribes directly or indirectly.

They had four children; the eldest was Shyamala, Shyamala Gopalan. Her younger sister Sarala is a retired obstetrician who lives in Chennai. She remained single and never married. Her youngest sister Mahalaxmi was an information scientist and worked for the government in Ontario, Canada. She got married but bore no children. Dr Balachandra Gopalan who is eighty now is younger to Shyamala. You can see that the entire family is modern, educated and cosmopolitan.

Isn't this story interesting? Yes, it is. Mr Gopalan was a married man, a family man. This used to an ideal number then.

Mother: Shyamala

Shyamala Gopalan is the mother of Kamala Devi Harris. In 2009 a reporter named Sam Whiting asked Kamala Harris a question:

"*Q. If your loft were on fire and you could only grab one thing, what would it be?*

A: Probably a photograph of me and my mother."

Shyamala Gopalan was born on 7 December 1938 in Madras. You have already seen that Shyamala's parents were intelligent enough to get their children educated. According to the standard of those days they were broad-minded in raising their children. Shyamala's early days were mostly spent in Delhi. She went to the Madrasi Education Association School, Mandir Marg (now part of the Delhi Tamil Education Association Schools) for her higher secondary education examination (1955). She was a gifted singer of Carnatic music and won a national competition in it as a teenager. She was invited to sing on All India Radio and got some fee for it also. She studied for a B.Sc. in Home Science at Lady Irwin College, a leading women's college in Delhi. I am sure Mr Gopalan as an intellectual and Tamil Brahmin elite wanted her eldest daughter to pursue a career in sciences. Lady Irwin College was founded by the British to provide an education in science to Indian women. She was forced to settle for Home Science.

In India, even today Home Science is a subject which gets less appreciation. Her brother Bala and father Gopalan used to tease her for her subject of study. They would say, "What do you study in Home Science? Do they teach you to set up plates for dinner?"

She knew what she was studying. She used to get irritated but always kept her cool as she had a future-plan. Her father thought deeply that his daughter should not get restricted to just homemaking courses. Mrs Rajam, the mother, also wanted her daughters to become doctors and engineers. Sensing her parents wish and desire Shyamala applied to a master's programme in nutrition and endocrinology at the University of California, Berkeley. She was a gifted student. Parents support was in full. She applied to a graduate programme at Berkeley, US, a university she'd never seen or heard about. But once she informed her parents about her selection, she was allowed to go and study. It was a fait accompli. She was a teenager. She was just 19. But she was brave enough to go. Her parents knew that it would be very hard for her to live there and it would also not be easy for them to arrange finances for her education. She told her father not to worry and left for her studies with perhaps a self-promise to return.

Deciding to leave her family behind in India was hard enough for Shyamala, coming to the United States as a teenager wouldn't have been any easier too. It is estimated that Indian Americans are about 40 lakhs. So many Indians from all parts of India go there regularly. There are new laws and policies and it isn't so difficult to travel. But Shyamala arrived at a time when discriminatory immigration laws placed severe quotas on Asian immigrants. The number of Indians allowed to move to the US was just 100 a year. It is also true that number of girls used just less than ten in number. When Shyamala reached the US, she must have found very few Indians around her. It is also true that she faced and felt racism and discrimination. She was an outsider and her chances of success largely depended on her personal qualities and dogged pursuits.

She was expected to return to India after she completed her degree. Mr Gopalan and his wife both must be thinking to settle their daughter according to Hindu traditions. But life keeps amazing secrets hidden from the sight of everyone. Shyamala too didn't know what was there in store for her.

"Kamala's family line was a strong black-and-brown braid coiling from India to Jamaica to Berkeley, California..." This is a well-written organic line from Nikki Grimes's book "Kamala Harris: Rooted in Justice". In fact, you will also appreciate; Kamala's family is a socio-political saga, focussing especially on three generations of immigrants.

This is the background when Kamala Harris addressed the viewers from the Chase Centre in Wilmington, a video featuring her sister, stepdaughter, and niece introduced her as a role model, a friend and a rock of stability for a large blended family. As she accepted the nomination, she knew that the unstinted support of her entire family was with her as ever. And when she acknowledged her family's support for her she included not only her immediate family, but also a lot many since the country's founding.

"That I am here tonight is a testament to the dedication of generation before me; Women and men who believed so fiercely in the promise of equality, liberty, and justice for all. We're not often taught their stories. But as Americans we all stand on their shoulders."

This slender book and a solitary chapter cannot hold so much. That is why I shall limit and restrict my narration. To commemorate the historic win, Kamala Harris gave a victory speech. In her speech, she said she was thinking of her mother and about "the generations of women, Black women, Asian, white, Latina, Native American women, who throughout our nation's history, have paved the way for this moment." Apart from her mother, she also shouted out to her family - her husband and two children, specifically - saying she loves them more than she could ever express. This wasn't unique for her, whose career has been shaped by the members of her family and her relationships with them. Here is an introductory profile of those who play a notable part in Kamala's life.

Maya: Sister

Maya was a top policy adviser for Hillary Clinton's 2016 presidential campaign and before that, the vice president for democracy, rights, and justice at the Ford Foundation and the executive director of the ACLU of Northern California. She finished undergraduate at the University of California-Berkeley and then law school at Stanford with her young daughter in tow before becoming one of the youngest-ever law school deans, at Lincoln Law School in San Jose, California, when she was just 29 years old. She'd go on to lead the American Civil Liberties Union of Northern California and earn a reputation as one of the most respected civil rights advocates in the country.

When you read her 2014 paper "Women of Colour: A growing Force in the American Electorate", you notice her erudite wisdom. "Women of colour will become full participants in the nation's democracy, ensuring a better public discourse for them, their families, and, ultimately, the country as a whole."She professed.

Maya is Kamala's younger sister. She has always been with her sister in thick and thin. When the opposition in politics is very violent and fierce, Kamala has been very lucky that she has a sister like her. In an article "Who is Kamala Harris, really? Ask sister Maya." by Ben Terris (The Washington Post, July 23,

2019), we get vivid account of Maya also who looked more like her mother than her father. Maya is about three years younger than Kamala. While she was just seventeen years of age and in school, she became a mother to her only child, Meena. Ben Terris has this to write about Maya as a teen-aged pretty girl.

> *"She was pretty (best-looking, according to her graduating yearbook), getting stellar grades and popular. And so no one seemed to notice anything was up as she made her way through senior year wearing bigger and chunkier sweatshirts (it was, after all, the '80s).*
>
> *"Nobody knew she was pregnant until she was about eight or nine months," recalled Judy Robinson, a close friend whose mother used to take care of the Harris sisters when Shyamala was away. Maya graduated from high school with honours, 17 years old, in her second trimester, and keeping a secret that even her closest friends didn't know about.*
>
> *Maya does not talk about this part of her life. Not the pregnancy. Not who the father was (other than to say he was never really in the picture). Not who she kept the secret from or for how long."*

She will talk about what came next: the birth of her daughter, Meena;

In 1998, she married Tony West, a lawyer. Maya Harris, like her sister, is a lawyer by profession. She has also been active in politics. Maya is an MSNBC political analyst and was named as one of three senior policy advisors in 2015 to guide the production of an agenda for the presidential campaign of Hillary Clinton in 2016. She was there at her sister's own brief presidential campaign in 2019.

She has always been seen at her sister's side since childhood. In an article on the Harris sisterhood published in

The Independent it was reported that Maya "has been dubbed "Bobby Kennedy" by their inner circle, by way of comparison with "the late politician's relationship with brother John F. Kennedy before becoming a political force himself." For Maya, her sister is a "Joyful warrior" and for Kamala, she is herself "big sister general". On National Sibling Day, Kamala reverted back to Maya's instagram caption, "I would not be the same person without my brilliant and thoughtful sister by my side." In an interview with The Washington Post, Kamala said of her relationship with Maya, "We forged a bond that is unbreakable. When I think about it, all of the joyous moments in our lives, all of the challenging moments, all of the moments of transition, we have always been together."

Here is a children's book "Superheroes". In this book Kamala Harris talks about her childhood days and her sister. She says, "My sister was a superhero because she was someone I could count on."

"My sister Maya and I did everything together- ballet class, piano lesson, like riding and board games. I knew that if I ever needed her, she'd be there, one half of our dynamic duo. When we felt sad, my mom would throw us an 'unbirthday party'. So we would feel better. Together, we'd eat un-birthday cake, open un-birthday presents, and dance around the living room. Maya was always by my side."

In another Children's book "Kamala and Maya's Big Idea" written by Maya's daughter you can find how Maya and Kamala got the big idea. What is this idea? Let us read:

"The big idea is to build a playground in the courtyard of their apartment building. The sisters take their idea to the landlord, who very quickly says no. But they're not quite willing to give up. Instead, they start spreading the idea to the other kids in the building. Kamala writes a persuasive

letter. Then she starts organizing volunteers. The girls are resourceful and persistent, and they learn that 'maybe' can be turned into 'yes' when people see there's a way forward."

Maya's daughter Meena got the idea of writing the book from her mother Maya and her aunt's Kamala age-old photograph. In the photo both of them looked as if they'd conquered the world. Meena is blessed with two daughters and this book is for them as well. But for us- the readers- the book is a peek in the minds of these two sisters. Maya Harris said in an interview with her daughter and sister, "We were always taught to stand up for ourselves, to stand up for others, to speak up."

Maya's husband

Derek Anthony West (born August 12, 1965) is an American attorney and former government official, and the Chief Legal Officer of Uber. He is responsible for its legal, security and compliance and ethics functions. Before Uber, he was Acting Associate Attorney General of the United States and general counsel of PepsiCo.

West attended Harvard University and Stanford Law School, where he was president of the "Stanford Law Review", only the third African-American person to hold the position. Maya and West were both in the class of 1992 at Stanford Law School. West has been married to Maya Harris since 1998. It is reported that West and Maya met at law school when her four year daughter, Meena, challenged him to a game of hide-and-seek. Maya and West were friends through law school and didn't start dating until after graduation, when he lived in Washington, DC, and she lived in the Bay Area.

When Kamala Harris was elected to the Senate in 2016, he co-led her transition team. It is rumoured that he will be very soon run for Attorney General.

Meena: an ambitious girl

Kamala Harris said during the 2020 Black Girls Lead conference, "There will be people who say to you, you are out of your lane. They are burdened by only having the capacity to see what has always been instead of what can be. But don't you let that burden you." Life of Meena Harris is the embodiment of all this.

Meenakshi Ashley Harris was born on October 20, 1984. Her mother is Maya Harris .Meena Harris is Kamala's dear niece and the only daughter of Maya. She attended Stanford as an undergraduate, then Harvard, where she received a J.D. She is also a lawyer by profession. She is also an author. She is married to Nikolas Ajagu. Meena has two cute daughters called Amara and Leela Ajagu. Her mother and aunt treated her like a little aunt when she was growing up in Oakland as an only child. Her mother and aunt treated her like a little adult. She said in an interview, "We never had a kiddy table. I knew that I came from a unique family." One can see how Meena also heeds the advice of her grandmother Shyamala Gopalan when she says, "You'll have people telling you that you're 'too young', 'too this', 'too that' and I saw my mom and aunt experiencing that in their professional careers. But consistent with what we were taught by my grandmother, they didn't take no for an answer."

Meena's mother Maya gave birth to her daughter when she was only seventeen years of age and still in high school. Kamala looked after Meena during evenings and weekends. Meena told all this in an interview with The Times. "Growing up, I was taught that ambition is something to celebrate, that it means purpose and determination, having a big idea and running after it, chasing your dreams and having confidence in yourself." She is all praise for Kamala and says, "She (Kamala Harris) has experienced her whole life- people said, "You're too young. You're too much of a woman. Frankly, you're too black. That's never been done before"."

In 2020, Meena Harris released her first children's book from HarperCollins entitled "Kamala and Maya's Big Idea", which is based on the real story of her mother, Maya Harris and aunt Kamala Harris. The main take away from the slender book are:

1. Little girls are powerful and capable of big bold things.
2. People may tell you know, or you're too little, or it's not possible, or it costs too much. But you should show perseverance in the face of barriers.
3. The girls of colour are leaders, who should follow, support and listen to.

She published "Ambitious girl" also. This book was published on January 19, 2021. In the book, a young girl takes advice from the women around her, including her mother and her grandmother, who teaches her the importance of growing up assertive, confident, and proud. Meena Harris said that listening to the dreams and career paths of other people is a good way to teach people how to embrace their own ambition. It shows that ambition isn't a "dirty" word and having dreams is not a "bad" thing.

This new children's book is inspired by the women who raised her—including her grandmother, mom Maya, and aunt Kamala Harris.

"I was raised to believe that ambition was a good thing. That it was something to be celebrated. It meant purpose, it meant power, it meant determination, it meant having a dream and going after it, even when other people tried to tell you it couldn't be done. That's all I knew, because my whole family was this little unit of me, my grandma, my mom, and my aunt, and it's what I would see every day."

Through this book Meena sets out to teach girls to reclaim, reframe, and redefine words like ambitious—as well as bossy, competitive, persistent, assertive, and loud—starting at a young age.

Meena's two young daughters Amara and Leela (note their Indian names) also look up to their great and famous aunt. You too would like a Video of Meena's daughter Amara in which Kamala Harris tells her, "You could be president. But not right now- you have to be over the age of 35." She never "sugarcoats" the reality of racism and sexism when talking to her kids.

I am tempted to quote from an article by Meena Harris. She wrote this piece for "Vogue" (22 June 2028) magazine. Disenchanted with the political mood in America, Meena Harris launched the Phenomenal Woman Action Campaign. *Phenomenal Woman is her grassroots initiative that promotes activism and empowers women.* She wrote "How to change the world, a five step guide". Here are the top five things that helped me to build a vibrant and engaged digital community.

1. Collaborative coalitions increase impact
2. It's not all about celebrity selfies
3. Online engagement is deepened by offline interaction
4. Thinking like an entrepreneur grows the movement
5. History provides important context

"When you inspire other people to do the same, you've created power that has the potential to elevate an entire community. It starts with identifying the issues you're passionate about and thinking creatively. And if you employ some of the strategies above, maybe you will even spark a movement." Meena has this to say to inspire us.

Let me take the liberty to add that Indians were not very happy when Meena spoke in favour of farmers' protest. She joined several international personalities in criticizing the crackdown on the farmers' movement in India. She tweeted:

> "It's no coincidence that the world's oldest democracy was attacked not even a month ago, and as we speak, the most populous democracy is under assault. This is related. We ALL should be outraged by India's internet shutdowns and paramilitary violence against farmer protesters.
>
> Militant nationalism is just as potent a force in US politics as it is in India or anyplace else. It can only be stopped if people wake up to the reality that FASCIST DICTATORS aren't going anywhere. Not unless: 1) we organize and 2) THERE ARE CONSEQUENCES FOR THE CAPITOL ATTACK."

Let me remind you, actually I needn't remind you, social activism has been a family affair for her. India is not only in her DNA, it's also in her thoughts. She is the daughter of Maya and granddaughter of Shyamala Gopalan. Her great grandmother was Mrs Rajam Gopalan. She grew up surrounded by "these strong and brilliant women who showed her what it meant to show up in the world with purpose and intention."

Maya Angelou's poems have always been an inspiration to her. It has been put on a branded tee-shirt by her. In the poem "Phenomenon Woman", the speaker refers to an elusive "secret" about herself that conventionally attractive women struggle to understand. She explains that she doesn't look like the models glorified by the fashion industry, and that when she stars to reveal her secret these other women don't believe her.

Pretty women wonder where my secret lies.

I'm not cute or built to suit a fashion model's size

But when I start to tell them,

They think I'm telling lies.

Here lies the secret of this ...

Yes, here lies the secret Meena taking active interest in Indian women. When she heard about Nodeep Kaur arrested on January 12, 2021 after a demonstration in Haryana's Kundali Area, Meena used her tweet to draw public attention to the arrest of a young Indian woman who was agitating against erratic wage payment.

There is a spirit of activism in whatever she does. She says, "I won't be silenced" and we Indians were alarmed. She wrote condemning, "Violent Hindu Extremism."

When we listen to her or read about her and carefully try to understand her views, we treat her not as an activist but as Kamala's niece. For us Vice President Kamala Harris is the first Indian-American to rise to such a position of power in American government.

Our concern couldn't go waste. According to a report in Los Angeles Times (February 11, 2021), Meena was cautioned by a White House legal team not to "build her brand" by using the name of the US Vice President. Her role as a social media influencer grabs the limelight. She told the New York Times Style section: "I'm my own person with my own views and my own platform and my own aspirations."

Balachandran Gopalan: Shyamala's brother

Kamala's maternal-uncle G. Balachandran lives in New Delhi. He is 80 years of age now. Mr Balachandran worked as a journalist before earning his master's degree in engineering. He earned a PhD in economics and computer science from the University of Wisconsin and worked in India. He married a Mexican woman named Rosamaria Orihuela. Balachandran's daughter, Sharada Balachandran Orihuela, is an associate professor of English and comparative literature at the University of Maryland.

When he heard the happy news about Kamala's feat, he was overjoyed and when Indian media contacted him to say a few words about her, this is what he said, "No doubt it is a proud moment for the whole family. We are quite happy that Kamala is the running mate of Joe Biden who hopes to be the US president." He is all praise for Kamala Harris. He terms Harris a "fighter". She is capable to overcome challenges and make herself heard. Bala said recollecting his life with his sister, "My sister has taught her to be brave." He wishes her good luck when he says, "I wish she does such a damn good job, four years later she will automatically get a Democratic nomination and win the presidency."

He lives in Delhi and is a former academic. He must have noticed what our Prime Minister tweeted and said about the 'historic occasion". But Bala's reaction according to reports was well-balanced, "They won't go out of the way to criticize India. What they won't do is give a carte blanche to India to do whatever it wants."

In a candid interview with rediff.com Shobha Warrier, the interviewer, asked Dr Bala a very simple question at the end of the interview. The question was, "Are you a proud uncle?" The answer was worth the weight of gold and I quote it in full.

"I am proud of her. There is no need to have greater pride now that she is the vice president. Then, I will have to have bigger pride when she becomes the president in four years time.

Yes, I am quite happy. Of course, I am proud and I will be after four years time too.

I was a proud uncle when she became the attorney general. I was a proud uncle when she became a senator.

I am a proud uncle today when she is the vice president and I will be a proud uncle when she becomes the president also. The feeling does not change."

Dr Sarala Gopalan: Shyamala's sister

Dr Sarala Gopalan is Shyamala's sister. She said, "I certainly feel it is my sister's upbringing and the values she taught Kamala since her childhood that has brought her where she is today. Her achievement makes all of us feel happy and proud. My sister herself was very progressive and brave. She went to the US alone 60 years ago to pursue to be brave and she has imbibed all the good qualities of my sister."

Sarala said that her sister Dr Shyamala had raised her daughters- Kamala and Maya –with good values and views which ensured they stuck to their roots. When Dr Shyamala Gopalan died in 2009, Kamala Harris flew down to Chennai to immerse her ashes in the Bay of Bengal and had remained in touch with her mother's family. She recalls that she flew to the US in 2017 when Harris was sworn-in as a senator. Dr Sarala Gopalan does not forget to mention to tell that Kamala loves South Indian cuisine. They are very fond of eating South Indian food.

During Kamala's race for California attorney general, she called her aunt Sarala Gopalan in Chennai and asked her to break coconuts for good luck at a Hindu temple overlooking the beach at Besant Nagar where she used to walk with her grandfather. The aunt lined up 108 coconuts to be offered.

Her aunt remembers about her (Kamala Harris) that she is a person who never forgets her roots and believes in family values. "Even today, she calls me chithi (mother's younger sister) and she has always been a caring person." Calling Kamala Harris a Diamond, Dr Sarala Gopalan said, "When she became a senator, I went to her and told her she was a diamond in the family. And she said to me, "Chitti, I am not a diamond in the family. I am a diamond among diamonds."

Sharada Balachandran Orihuela: First Cousin

Sharada Balachandran Orihuela is the daughter of Balachandran Gopalan. She is an English professor at the University of Maryland. She attended the ceremony and was pictured with Harris. I could gather some more information about her when I sneaked into her facebook profile and saw a photograph in which Kamala and Sharada were together. For an Indian like me these names are venerable. These are the names of the deities I worship in the temple. I am a Hindu and for me it is a daily routine. Sharada and Kamala (or Balachandran Orihuela and Kamala Harris,) are two great persons in their own fields of activity. Those who know something about Indian family and relationship they will understand better than others that Kamala and Sharada both had grown up in a family with roots in India and branches in several other countries. It must have been very complicated and difficult. Sharada was right when she told Liam Farrell (Maryland Today), "I had just grown up in this family with all its complexities and its Diasporas. It's only as an adult that I realize how wild it is." You can also sense it that Sharada's life must have been amazing. Her father is an Indian and mother Rosamaria Orihuela was a Mexican. She must have got the lessons in family values from so many sources and balancing each one must have been a tremendous task.

She recollects those days when she lived with Shyamala as an undergraduate at Oakland's Mills College. That was the time after 9/11 terrorist attacks. Shyamala warned her that American men would call her exotic but she shouldn't bother. She said, "The minute they call you exotic, you walk away from them and tell them to F---K off."

For Sharada, Kamala is the cousin who took her to her first punk rock concert. "To me, she's just my cousin who came over to dinner," she said in an interview to Maryland Today. "She almost belongs to everybody now."

Sharada is an author of many academic books. She authored the 2018 book, *"Fugitive, Smugglers, and Thieves: Piracy and Personhood in American Literature."*

Donald Harris: Father

Donald Jasper Harris, Kamala's father, was born on August 23, 1938 in Brown's Town, St. Ann Parish, and Jamaica. He is a Jamaican economist and professor emeritus at Stanford University. He is well-known for applying post-Keynesian Ideas to development economics. Harris arrived at the University of California, Berkeley on a colonial Jamaican government scholarship in the fall of 1961.

In an essay about his Jamaican ancestry, He writes about a Hamilton in his family. "My roots go back, within my life-time, to my personal grandmother, Miss Chrishy (Christiana Brown, descendant of Hamilton Brown who is on record as plantation and slave owner and founder of Brown's town.) Though Mr Brown was a slave-trader, he had got himself high-positions and was a member in the House of Assembly. He was also an attorney, agent, assignee, executor, guardian, manager, receiver, or trustee for more than fifty estates. Historian Christer Petley in his book "Slave-holders in Jamaica" writes that in Jamaica there were more than fifty estates and more than two hundred enslaved people. I needn't delve deep into this as it is not required.

Donald J. Harris moved to the United States in the 1960s to get his Ph.D. at the University of California-Berkeley. He later became naturalized as a U.S. citizen. Harris taught at the University of Illinois and Northwestern University briefly, and then became an associate professor at the University of Wisconsin-Madison before moving to California and securing a job as a Professor of Economics at Stanford University. Now, after retiring in the late 1990s, he holds the title of emeritus professor. He was a left-leaning iconoclast who wrote and taught about uneven economic development around the world, particularly across racial lines, long before many Americans had ever heard the phrase 'income inequality'. Colleagues found his progressivism threatening - he was called "too charismatic, a pied piper leading students away from neoclassical economics," in The Stanford Daily. According to Mr Harris's Stanford bio, "His research and publications have centred on exploring the analytical conception of the process of capital accumulation and its implications for a theory of growth of the economy, with the aim of providing thereby an explanation of the intrinsic character of growth as a process of *uneven* development."

He must be very happy to know about his daughter's achievement but when he wrote in a column for *Jamaica Mother Global Online*, we understood his state of mind. He wrote, "Speaking for myself and my immediate Jamaican family, we wish to categorically dissociate ourselves from the travesty." Like Shyamala, he too was a very intelligent and brilliant student. He studied Economics at the University of California at Berkeley. He taught Economics at Stanford University where he still remains a professor emeritus.

Ms Harris wrote in her autobiography and also in the book for Children.

> "*My dad wanted me to be fearless. Whenever we were at the park, he'd let go of my hand and call out, "Run, Kamala, run!" and I'd run as far as I could for as long as I could.*"

In a 2018 essay published via Jamaica Global Online, Dr Harris underlined his philosophy of life, "Remember where you come from."(member whey u cum fram). I am sure Ms Harris must have also received her father's teachings at some point of her life. He wanted to make sure his children understood their father's homeland of Jamaica. He and Shyamala fell in love protesting. Kamala Harris in her book "The Truths we hold" writes about accompanying them to demonstrations while she was in a stroller. She writes that her mother and father "stopped being kind to each other" by the time she was 5. In 1971, when Kamala was 7, the two divorced. "It was hard on both of them. I think, for my mother, the divorce represented a kind of failure she had never considered."

In an article "The Jamaican Connection" published in The Washington Post (January 17, 2021) Robert Samuels writes about Kamala Harris's father who is a proud islander who made sure his daughters knew their heritage.

When Kamala Harris got a little older, her father introduced her to Marley and Jimmy Cliff. She picked up some patois, the distinct Jamaican dialect that blends English with African languages. He also tried to shape an understanding of the culture that went beyond food and music. He taught his daughters about the history of Jamaican Maroons, kidnapped Africans who rebelled from their captors and escaped to the mountains. The elder Harris taught her about the vast gulf between the wealthy and the poor in Jamaica, and the challenges to economic growth –blending his experience with his expertise.

While Kamala Harris is very forthcoming about her Indian roots, she talks less about her Jamaican roots. She doesn't talk about her father very often. The reason is very simple. Her father and her mother got separated. When Kamala was seven years of age and her sister hardly three; their parents had to fight custody battle in the family court of Oakland. When we have sweet-bitter memories, we tend to recollect less.

It would not be out of place and in bad taste to tell you about a joke Kamala made about her Jamaican roots. This was criticized by her father Dr Harris. It is reported that during an appearance on the radio show "The Breakfast Club", Kamala Harris joked with host Charlamagne tha God about her views on marijuana use. When asked whether she supported or opposed the legalization of the drug, she replied saying, "Half my family is from Jamaica. Are you kidding me?"

Her father Dr Harris was not happy hearing this. He reacted very sharply. He was so unhappy that he published a statement to Jamaica Global Online, "My dear departed grandmothers (whose extraordinary legacy I described in a recent essay on this website), as well as my deceased parents, must be turning in their grave right now to see their family's name, reputation and proud Jamaican identity being connected, in any way, jokingly or not with the fraudulent stereotype of a pot-smoking joy seeker and in the pursuit of identity politics."

Douglas Craig Emhoff: Husband

Douglas Craig Emhoff (born October 13, 1964) is an American lawyer who is the second gentleman of the United States. As the first-ever husband of a U.S. vice president, Emhoff is the first second gentleman in American history. "I might be the first, but I won't be the last" he commented recently.

He is also the first Jewish spouse of a vice president. By profession, he is an entertainment lawyer. Emhoff was married for 16 years to Kerstin Emhoff, née Mackin. They have two children, Cole and Ella.

They met on a blind date in 2013, set up by Harris' good friend Chrisette Hudlin, a public relations consultant. Hudlin and her husband arranged a meeting with Emhoff about a knotty legal issue, which they ended by asking if he was single. She told Emhoff about Harris, then-California attorney general and her friend of 30 years.

In a CNN interview (January 15, 2021) Doug Emhoff and Kamala Harris recalled their first date. He narrated, "It felt like we had known each other for ever. I didn't want it to end. And so the next morning, I pulled the move of emailing her with my availabilities for the next four months, including long weekends. And I said something like, "I'm too old to hide the ball. You're great. I want to see if we can make this work. Here's when I'm available next. And I guess it worked." He is the man who could make her laugh. As the instruction given to Kamala by her mother was "Life will have its ups and downs, so you make sure that you find a life partner who makes you laugh." she accepted the proposal.

Kamala was about 50 years of age when she got married. They married in 2014 at a Santa Barbara, California, courthouse when they were both two months shy of 50 years old. (Their birthdays are a week apart.) It's unconventional but true. Even popular Bollywood and Hollywood may not dare to take up such a script. I have read somewhere that she googled for Douglas even though her best friend who 'set them up' asked not to. Douglas didn't know that Kamala had googled him for years. Instagram told me this:

> "*Kamalaharris – When your friend tells you not to Google him before your first blind date.*
>
> *I did.*"

He married Kamala Harris on August 22, 2014, in Santa Barbara, California, with Kamala's sister Maya Harris officiating. They were married in a ceremony incorporating both Indian and Jewish traditions. He wore a flower garland around his neck to honour Kamala's Indian heritage. At the end, they smashed a glass per Emhoff's Jewish tradition. It was a ritual of compromise in pursuit of unity; an exchange of promises. This day Douglas Emhoff became the man who captured her heart for ever. And since then, all they have looked back on are memories of fun and frolic. He is now 'a father, hubby, lawyer, and a wannabe golfer."

Kamala Harris is always careful when she talks about her family. She is ever thankful to each one of them. In her victory speech as the vice president-elect, she spoke volumes about her husband, lawyer Doug Emhoff, his two kids, Cole and Ella Emhoff. The Washington Post published the story of Kamala and Doug, a match made in Hollywood (literally).The official website states that Douglas Emhoff, the husband of Vice President Kamala Harris is a devoted father, experienced lawyer, and proud husband.

It is interesting to note that Ms Kamala Harris has dedicated her autobiography "The Truths We Hold: An American Journey" to him and the words used are really great.

"To my darling husband:

Thank you for always being patient, loving, supportive, and calm. And most of all, for your sense of "the funny"."

Even the autobiography begins with a scene in which the husband and wife begin their day.

"Most mornings, my husband Doug, wakes up before me and reads the news in bed. If I hear him making noises – a sigh, a groan, a gasp- I know what kind of day it's going to be ..."

Let me add what our own Shashi Tharoor says about the second gentleman, "While many women are relishing the prospect of the US getting used to Harris' husband, Douglas Emhoff, in the unprecedented role of being the first "second gentleman", the fact is that from Denis Thatcher to Asif Ali Zaradri, men around the world have played such a role and adjusted easily to its challenges."

Let me also tell you that he got the title of the first ever male spouse of a vice president and the word "second gentleman" has been added to the Merriam Webster dictionary. "Second gentleman' is defined as "the husband or male partner of a Vice president or second in command of a country or jurisdiction." The first known use of the term was found in 1976. "Well, now it's official. I might be the first, but I won't be the last." He tweeted.

Doug Emhoff is showing America how male partners can gracefully take a step back from their own professions to uplift the careers of the women in their lives. He is no longer working for DLA and will focus on his new role as second gentleman. He will also teach a class at Georgetown University Law Centre. He wrote in an essay for GQ, "I want my kids to grow up in a world where it isn't news that a loving partner, – of any gender, supports them in everything they do."

As I recollect and collect that he has a role that has no job description, no salary, and no formal duties. He is a spouse and is going to do something exemplary. Traditionally, first and second ladies have played the role of hostess: decorating for the holidays, presiding over luncheons, submitting family recipes to a magazine's annual "first Lady Cookie Contest", etc. One thing is certain. He is going to support her.

The marriage between Kamala and Emhoff will pave the way and many Black women will get a chance to re-examine a racial taboo that has shaped many of their private lives. Many Black women have traditionally avoided White men for a variety of reasons. Similarly Some Asian women are wary of being with White men for some of the same reasons as Black women. In 2015, one in ten married people in the US had a spouse of a different race or ethnicity, according to a Pew Research Centre Study. But in reality there are many Black women who don't want to compromise. They are inspired by examples such as Michelle Obama's marriage and they want what she seems to have – a Black man they can respect and love. Now it will be easy to cite Kamala Harris's marriage as an inspirational model for all people who say colour doesn't matter. Black women who are scared of dating White men should pay attention to Emhoff and see for themselves how he treats Kamala Harris.

Cole and Ella: Momala

Kamala Harris is stepmother to two children. They are Cole and Ella Emhoff. They were named after John Coltrane and Ella Fitzerald. The children and the mother agreed they didn't like the term "stepmom". These children call her "Momala". This word is a combination of two words. In Yiddish language we have a word "Mamelah" which means "little mother". So Kamala and Momala becomes "Momala" for the kids. Her children call her "Momala" and she herself is of the view that this title is very important to her. We can find this word in her Twitter bio. Harris called Cole and Ella her "endless source of love and pure joy" (May 2019 Elle essay). She says one thing with certainty that her heart wouldn't be whole, nor her life full, without them. "They are brilliant, talented, funny kids who have grown to be remarkable adults. I was already hooked on Doug, but I believe it was Cole and Ella who reeled me in." Kamala Harris wrote.

When you read an article "On Being Momala" written by Kamala Harris and published in ELLE (May 10, 2019), you get what it's like to be a stepmom – or, as her kids call her "Momala". So true, indeed!

When you have a family and members of family are your vocal supporters, it becomes difficult to avoid some criticism. Kamala Harris may face questions in future about her relatives and members of her family profiting from their relationship. Those who are distant relatives or live in India may not give her any problem, but those around her may cause annoyance. When it was heard that her daughter received a modelling contract a week after Inauguration Day, people felt awkward. The sale of Harris-themed clothes and merchandise is also being seen as an endorsement. One can't avoid such things.

"The Vice President and her family will uphold the highest ethical standards and it's the White House's policy that the

Vice President's name should not be used in connection with any commercial activities that could reasonably be understood to imply an endorsement or support," vice presidential spokeswoman Sabrina Singh said in a statement.

Let us also not forget what she wrote in her memoir, "We sometimes joke that our modern family is almost too functional."

◘

6. Experiments with the Truth

'A patriot is not someone who condones the conduct of our country whatever it does. It is someone who fights every day for the ideals of the country, whatever it takes.'

—Kamala Harris

Vice President Kamala Harris is also an author of three books. She has written an inspiring memoir and an illustrated children's book. She has got many firsts but as an author she is not the first VP who authored a book. She writes for the people. In her memoir, "The Truths We Hold" she writes about the "nerves, excitement, and adrenaline" running through her mind the first time she said those words as prosecutor.

For the people

Every school boy knows the definition of democracy by Abraham Lincoln. He connected democracy's preservation with 'a new birth of freedom' and he appears to have defined the word "democracy" in direct opposition to slavery. In his Gettysburg Address, he extolled the sacrifices of those who died at Gettysburg and exhorted his listeners to resolve:

"That these dead shall not have died in vain-that this nation, under God, shall have a new birth of freedom- and that government of the people, by the people, for the people, shall not perish from the earth."

In just 271 words, beginning with the now iconic phrase "Four score and seven years ago" referring to the signing of the Declaration of Independence, he created magic. Can the magic he created be recreated by a tweet consisting of 280 characters?

Now, let me not beat about the bush. I come to the point straightaway. History isn't about dates and eras. It's about people- their beliefs, their actions, the relationship and understanding and the choices we make with our valuable lives. The past is a foreign country, a fascinating one, where human choices, human beliefs and human relationships mingle with each other and create a beautiful rainbow of unity in diversity. In the end what matters is "the people"- "We the People".

Kamala Harris picked up the phrase "for the people" to associate herself with that tradition and took a pledge to preserve and protect it. She speaks like a leader, not more not less. When she was district attorney, she realized what exactly "for the people" meant. While training her younger lawyers, she'd say, "Let's be clear. You represent the people. So I expect you to get to know exactly who the people are…For the people means for them. All of them."

When she stood before the DNC delegates and accepted the nomination to be Joe Biden's running mate almost 100 years from the day that the 19th Amendment gave women the right to vote, she stood up to make history. In her acceptance speech, she remembered those who fought to have a voice, a vote and a seat at the table.

"These women picked up the torch and fought on" she said in her acceptance speech, "As Americans, we all stand on their shoulders."

Kamala Harris has spent her entire life defending her country's cherished values. From fighting to fix broken criminal justice system to taking on the Wall Street banks for middle-class homeowners, she has always worked for the people. She understands her responsibility to represent demands of the people who ushered her into office of the VP.

The White House web-site also informs the reader: Kamala Harris, the vice president… A career for the people- breaking barriers and fighting for working families…

Her tweeter account is Kamala Harris- Vice President of the United States, Wife, Momala, and Auntie. Fighting for the people… She / her.

Linked.in profile created by her also includes these words.

Her campaign slogan, "For the People" is the phrase she used to formally announce her appearances as a prosecutor in the California superior courts. What more to say? Yes, plenty. And she puts it bluntly in her memoir.

"Put bluntly, we have work to do. Hard work. Indispensible work. We have everything we need- all the raw ingredient- to build an economy for the twenty first century that is fair and sturdy, an economy that rewards the work of those who sustain it. But we have to hurry. And we have to be willing to speak truth."

The father of India, Mahatma Gandhi, lead a life in which the truth, ultimate truth remained the key that opened all doors. The word *satya* (Truth) is derived from Sat which means 'being'. Nothing is or exists in reality except Truth. That is why Satya or Truth is perhaps the name of God. In fact, it is more correct to say that Truth is God than to say God is Truth. But as we cannot do without a ruler or a general, such names of God as "king" or "kings" or "The Almighty" are and will remain generally current. On deeper thinking, however it will be realized that Sat or Satya is the only correct and full sign fact name for God. The Idea of Truth and its reality has been the biggest victim of our times.

Whatever Gandhi wrote in his autobiography "My Experiments with Truth", Kamala Harris wrote in her autobiography in a different way. Writing about the truth in the age when the idea of truth has become the biggest victim of our time is not an easy task. Nobody cares about it anymore. Perhaps it requires a Gandhi to have the courage to speak the truth and stand for the truth. Kamala, the daughter of India, spoke the truth in the time of liars. Her autobiography "The Truths We Hold: An American Journey" (2019) is rightly being compared to Barack Obama's memoirs "Dreams from My Father" and "The Audacity of Hope". A reviewer, Danielle Kurtzleben, treats it as a campaign book and finds in it some ulterior motive. But she also accepts its effectiveness. Kamala's prose may not be Pulitzer worthy but it is effective and reaches the heart. Her campaign slogan reaches the audience, "Kamala Harris, for the people".

The Truths We Hold

The book according to the author is a collection of ideas, viewpoints, and stories from her life, much of it spent in public service, and the many people she has met over the years. It will take you through a life lived among people of strong characters and convictions. The book introduces the people who have played important roles in her life. It gives an idea of the experiences that have shaped her as the politician and possible future president of the US.

The Truths We Hold is a saga of Kamala Harris's personal and professional life in 10 chapters. She presents herself as a progressive prosecutor. She is of the view that every criminal doesn't need punishment. They instead should be helped by the law of the land. In her book Kamala Harris speaks clearly on the burning topics including the Black Lives Matter movement.

The immediate purpose of the book may be presenting her in the best possible way but after the great whirlwind, the book is worth going through once again. Look at the hypothesis of the book in the preface of the book:

"We need to speak truth: that racism, sexism, homophobia, transfobia, and anti-Sematism are real in this country, and we need to comfort those forces. We need to speak the truth: that, with the exception of Native Americans, we all descend from people who weren't born on our shores – whether our ancestors came to America willing, with hopes of a prosperous future, or forcibly, on a slave ship, or desperately, to escape a harrowing past.

We must speak truth about our mass incarceration crisis- that we put more people in prison than any country on earth, for no good reason. We must speak truth about police brutality, about racial biases, about the killing of unarmed black men. We must speak truth about pharmaceutical companies that pushed addictive opioids on unsuspecting communities and payday lenders and fro-profit colleges that have leeched on to vulnerable Americans and overloaded them with debt. We must speak truth about greedy, predatory corporations that have turned deregulation, financial speculation, and climate denialism into creed. And I intend to do just that."

And she speaks the truth about so many things. She speaks that police brutality occurs in America. Police officials are rarely punished for their crimes. She writes in her autobiography, "Make no mistake: we need to take on this and every aspect of our broken criminal justice system. We need to change our laws and our standards. And we need to elect people who will make it their mission to do so."

Sharp on Justice

Kamala Harris has been a prosecutor for so many years. She knows the value of words. It is said in the law that anything one says or does can and will be held against him or her. She also knows that she should be very careful about what she says. Still she likes to use only one word-Truth.

"I'm a career prosecutor," Kamala Harris told the New York Times, "I have been trained and my experience over decades is to make decisions after a review of the evidence and the facts. And not to jump up with grand gestures before I have done that. Some might interpret that as being cautious, I would tell you that's just responsible."Kamala Harris is an assertive, strong and daring leader. She used her prosecutorial skills to make the opponents blink. She called Secretary of Homeland Security John Kelly on his home phone when she learned of the executive order banning travel from Muslim countries. She performed same-sex marriages in San Francisco under Mayor Gavin Newsom in 2004. She went after big banks.

She has been repeatedly saying that today's issues don't have to have an "either/or" option. In her memoir she writes:

"For too long, we'd been told there were only two options: to be either tough on crime or soft on crime- an oversimplification that ignored the realities of public safety. You can want the police to stop crime in your neighbourhood and also want them to stop using racing profiling. You can believe in the need for consequence and accountability, especially for serious criminals, and also oppose unjust incarceration. I believed it was essential to weave all these varied strands together."

She notes in the final chapter of her book that the key to winning an argument, in politics as in law, is to "show the math" –not just the bottom line.

Smart on Crime

She is very pragmatic. She is of the view that prisoners deserve the second chance. As the prisoners re-enter the society therefore we need to do what we can to keep them from committing crimes again and again. As I understand she treats punishment as a means to end the crime. She argues that focus on punishment has caused to lose sight of the goal of crime prevention. During her run for the Attorney General's post, she presented herself as a prosecutor who supported criminal justice reform. Recidivism and truancy are the pillars of her argument. She presents a clear and optimistic plan for crime prevention and reduction of recidivism. She says at the very outset, "Crime and optimism do not always go hand in hand. But optimism and problem solving are part of my DNA."

Kamala Harris shows that being "tough with crime" or being "soft with crime" is of no use, we should be "smart on crime". Smartness is her sutra. "Soft" and "tough" are "false choices". We are surrounded with false choices. She shows that the need to be "too darn serious" or "too darn perfect" is just another false choice.

"*Smart on Crime: A Career Prosecutor's Plan to Make Us Safer*" (2009) is a book by Kamala Harris with Joan O'C Hamilton. The book outlines her vision of how the criminal justice system should function. She explains in detail why it is not enough to simply be tough on crime and how prosecutors and lawmakers must also be smart and reformed-minded in their approach. She argues such changes would increase public safety, reduce costs, and strengthen communities.

She was a criminal prosecutor for so long, and then Attorney General (which is like the *capo di tutti capi* of all prosecutors). This shows that her grip on crimes and criminals is tough. When she wrote *Smart on Crime*, she was in the midst of a run for California attorney general, her first run for state-wide office. On the campaign trail in 2019, Kamala calls herself a "progressive prosecutor" whose goal was to change the system rather than perpetuate an inherently racist system. She portrays herself as a Drug Warrior: "Drug crimes exact a terrible toll and rob people young and old of hope," she intones in the book's introduction. Phrases like that scream hoarsely, "Watch out! Conservative nearby!" But since announcing for the presidency, Kamala has changed her attitude on the Drug War, asserting that marijuana "gives a lot of people joy, and we need more joy in the world" (For example, Washington Post, Feb. 11, 2019). In her 2019 book, The Truths We Hold, she writes, "America has a deep and dark history of people using the power of the prosecutor as an instrument of injustice -- of innocent men framed, of charges brought against people of colour without sufficient evidence, of prosecutors hiding information that would exonerate defendants."

Superheroes Are Everywhere

Kamala Harris examines the people and values that shaped her life from childhood onwards. She urges kids to be superheroes too, by being kind, brave, and curious, and by treating people fairly, sharing, and lending a hand when people need help. "You're a hero by being the very best YOU" is the central theme of the 40 page book "Superheroes Are Everywhere". It is apparent that it is a "Children's book" published exactly on January 8, 2019. It teaches that superheroes can be found everywhere in real life. We can find them among members of the family, friends, teachers at in school and college. Each page of the book proclaims something about heroes, e.g. "Heroes are kind".

Now that we are going to come to a close, understanding Kamala Harris in a childlike manner will be a good idea. It is a thumbnail biography of the VP of the US. People in her life who were superheroes in their own way because, like superheroes in stories, they made her feel special (mom), were people she could count on (sister), made her feel brave (dad), stood up for what's right (grandparents), made her feel safe (friends), helped show her the world and chase her dreams (teachers), were kind (neighbours), helped her explore (aunts and uncles), worked hard (mom, uncle, aunt), protected people (lawyers who were her role models), and made a difference in her life. This is what she meant by superheroes. The term can be applied to her too. I wish that you should also find around you your superheroes.

For many girls and boys Kamala Harris has become a sort of superhero. A group of young children sang a poem and congratulated the VP of the US.

Brown girl Brown girl, what do you see?

I see a Vice-President that looks like me.

Brown brown girl, what do you do?

I fought I hoped I spoke what was true.

Brown girl Brown girl, what do you know?

That there are strong women that want me to grow…

This is a modern take on a children's' book called, "Brown bear Brown bear, what do you see?" which was written by Eric Carle and Bill Martin Jr. This poem is penned by a Chicago-based poetess named Lesle Honore. Amanda Gorman too recites a poem. *The Hill We Climb* encapsulated the inherent diversity in unity reminding people of the America that was and one that will be:

We the successors of a country and a time

Where a skinny Black girl

Descended from slaves and raised by a single mother

Can dream of becoming president…

I am not a soothsayer but an Indian who believes in astrology. When I read frequent invocation and poems like these, I can also foretell that Kamala Devi Harris is going to be the next President of the United States.

The new dawn blooms as we free it

For there is always light

If only we're brave enough to see it

If only we're brave enough to be it…

7. I am who I am

'What I want young women and girls to know is: You are powerful and your voice matters. You're going to walk into many rooms in your life and career where you may be the only one who looks like you or who has had the experiences you've had. But you remember that when you are in those rooms, you are not alone. We are all in that room with you applauding you on. Cheering your voice. And just so proud of you. So you use that voice and be strong.'

—Kamala Harris

Donald Trump has been a house-hold name in India too. Trump and Modi were well-attended by both Indians and Indian Americans and the "Howdy Modi!" community summit in Houston drew crowds of about 50000 people. In America, he was the staunch adversary for Kamala Harris and her party. When Kamala Harris was campaigning, this name used to be on her lips. But it is strange that she didn't use even the word Trump in her memoir. It appears only once and even then it's a part of a quotation. It doesn't mean that he was not in her mind. It was since 2016 when Trump became the President. People read with interest now what Kamala said in an interview with "Vogue" four years ago. She recalled sitting on the couch after Donald Trump had been elected president and thinking,

This. Can't. Be. Happening.

Really, it was unprecedented. Donald Trump was an anomaly.

Let me tell you an interesting story. In 2016, when Alexander, Kamala's nine year old godson, saw Trump winning the presidential election that was under way, he asked her, "Auntie Kamala…that man can't win. He's not going to win. Is he?"

His words broke Kamala's thumping heart. She didn't want anyone making a child feel that way. She assured the boy that, like the "best superheroes" they would fight back. *Picture abhi baki hai*!

Let me quote it from Kamala Harris's memoirs. Perhaps her words and narration will make it more poignant and worth remembering.

"Come here, little man. What's wrong?"

Alexander looked up and locked eyes with mine. His voice was trembling. "Auntie Kamala, that man can't win. He's not going to win, is he?"

Alexander's worry broke my heart. I didn't want anyone making a child feel that way. Eight years earlier, many of us had cried tears of joy when Barack Obama was elected president. And now, to see Alexander's fear…

His father, Reggie, and I took him outside to try to console him.

"Alexander, you know how sometimes superheroes are facing a big challenge because a villain is coming for them? What do they do when that happens?"

"They fight back," he whimpered.

"That's right. And they fight back with emotion, because all the best superheroes have big emotions just like you. But they always fight back, right? So that's we're going to do."

That was the day when Kamala Harris became a U.S. senator-elect, the first black woman from her state and the second in the nation's history. She was elected to represent more than thirty-nine million people.

They fought back and the picture changed within four years. After 4 years she posted to her social media.

"We did it, we did it Joe. You're going to be the next President of the United States!"

This became one of the ten top tweets of 2020. An Indian like you and I read in it an invisible sentence.

"And I'm going to be the next Vice President."

Kamala Devi Harris makes history as first woman and woman of colour as Vice President of the United States of America. She "creates history". The Sunday Express reported with the headline: "Finally." The news was here, there and every nook and corner of India. She is "India's daughter", Indians proclaimed. Indians are exclaiming in unison, "This is a big moment for all of us. No doubt about it."

In her victory speech, she gave everyone hope and something wonderful to cheer about, Kamala Harris said this to all the girls of her country:

"While I may be the first woman in this office, I will not be the last. Every little girl watching tonight sees that this is a country of possibilities. And to the children of our country, regardless of your gender, our country has sent you a clear message: Dream with ambition, lead with conviction, and see yourselves in a way that others may not simply because they've never seen it before. But know that we will applaud you every step of the way."...

Every little girl and every small boy, even those who are grown up, will appreciate that this book is a story of the person who made a name for herself, her family and each one of us. It is the remarkable story Ms Harris told a part of it repeatedly during her campaign trails. It is the story frequently told by Western media. It is the story that holds the truth and has been told by her in her inspiring autobiography "The Truths We Hold".

On January 20, 2021 Joe Biden and his running mate, Kamala Devi Harris, were sworn in as President and Vice president of the United States. She had been the first many times before. She had been the first Black woman district attorney in California. She had been the first Black woman senator from California.

In other words, Kamala has steadily moved up in ranks since her time at the San Francisco District Attorney's office in the 1990s. She became San Francisco's District Attorney in 2004. Then she was elected as California Attorney General in 2010 and was re-elected to the post in 2014. Her entire career has been focused on helping people to remain safe and sound. In November 2016, she ran for the senate and became the third female from California and the first of either Indian or Jamaican descent to become a senator. I can foresee that her legacy will create an atmosphere of goodwill and a far easier pathway than before for other persons of colour and women. It is certain that her victory is going to shatter so many barriers for women set by American political culture.

"Where Do We Go from Here?" More than fifty years ago, Martin Luther King Jr. raised this question. In his 1967 book "Where Do We Go from Here: Chaos or Community" Nobel Prize laureate, social justice campaigner, and non-violent as Gandhi MKL or Martin Luther King Jr. advocated for human rights and a sense of hope for all. The question has been a constant feature of African American politics since then.

By emphasizing the Vice President's blackness, I do not mean to erase her South Asian Heritage. I'm simply acknowledging that most Americans see her as Black. The public discourse in America takes Kamala Harris and her identity as a Black woman because she has written about herself as a Black woman (see her autobiography, 2019). Her dual background as South Asian and Black are mutually inclusive. I think her being Asian doesn't mean she is not Black. I do not think her being Black means she is not Asian. In fact, she is in her own way trying to present an answer of the question...

The official website of the White House mentions Kamala Harris THE VICE PRESIDENT, a career for the people-breaking barrier and fighting for working families. "Throughout her career, the Vice President has been guided by the words she spoke the first time she stood up in court: Kamala Harris, for the people... She is the first woman, the first Black American, and the first South Asian American to be elected Vice President, as was the case with other offices she has held. She is, however, determined not to be the last."

https://www.whitehouse.gov/administration

We, Indians, rejoice in Kamala Harris's outstanding achievement in the US. Manisha Sinha, history professor at the University of Connecticut says that Harris's vice-presidency has galvanised huge enthusiasm among Black women and the Indian American and Asian American communities which signifies, "a new direction in American democracy." It has taken 55 years after the Immigration and Nationality Act of 1965 for the first Indian American woman to be chosen on the national ticket as a President running mate. It took 244 years after American independence and 100 years since the Suffragette Moment to secure a right to vote from women in this age of global feminist movements.

She is the proud daughter of an Indian mother, a daughter of immigrants, and we, Indians, are proud to know that she has risen so high and reached where no woman ever reached. This is a unique achievement. She has broken through "the glass ceiling".

"Many women of colour could relate not only to Harris's personal experiences as the daughter of immigrants and her use of words like "chittis", a Tamil term of endearment, but to the challenges she faced on the campaign like being interrupted by Vice President Mike Pence on the debate stage or having to silence birtherism rumours," said Sayu Bhojwani, founder and president of New American Leaders, New York City's first commissioner of immigrant affairs and founder of South Asian Youth Action.

"To watch her overcome that is a win for all of us," she said. "Her election widens the lens for who an American leader can be." Karthick Ramakrishnan, a political science professor at the University of California-Riverside pointed out that Harris, one of five Indian American senators, is part of a trend of the community gaining political power and increasing civic participation faster than groups like Chinese and Japanese Americans.

Lakshmi Puri, former assistant secretary-general of the United Nations and deputy executive director of UN Women, in her glorious article "Yes, She can" (Indian Express, Nov 16, 2020) puts Kamala's feat very brilliantly, "Harris's elevation to VP pushes the frontiers of diversity. Notably, she is the first biracial (South Asian and African), intercultural (Indian and Jamaican), interfaith (Hindu and Baptist) woman and daughter of immigrant parents to hold this post. Her husband, Douglas Emhoff (white and Jewish), is the first "second-gentleman" and their "modern blended family" is a new role model. Hence, Harris represents intersectional feminism in an increasingly multicultural pluralistic America."

We have not forgotten that the US has actually been rather several decades behind in electing women to high office. Nearly 100 years to this day after the ratification of the Nineteenth Amendment which granted American women suffrage so many of the black women were still prohibited from voting. There are only a handful of them such as Shirley Chisholm who inspired Ms Harris "to pick up the torch and go on." It is believed that without Shirley Chisholm they would have been no Barack Obama and no Kamala Harris. No woman has made it to the Oval Office or gone so far before Kamala Devi Harris. She made it as her commitment, to quote the Holy Bible, "to walk by faith, and not by sight" and saying, "I am here today because of the women who came before me."

So far so good, better late than never…

American: I am who I am.

"Though we may be physically separated, we, the American people are united in spirit." Kamala Harris, Facebook post 21st January 2021."

Kamala Harris is a multiracial American and a Baptist, holding membership of the Third Baptist Church of San Francisco, a congregation of the American Baptist Churches USA. Notwithstanding her background, she has always been comfortable with her identity and describes herself as an "American". She told The Washington Post in 2019 that politicians should not have to fit into compartments because of their colour or background. "My point was: I am who I am. I'm good with it. You might need to figure it out. But I'm fine with it."

We, Indians, say that unity in diversity is the salutary quality of Indian polity. Those who go to the US for different reasons they also find that in the schools and colleges, workplaces and markets there is a rainbow of different colours and people. America is also diverse and though Whites are about 63 percent, there are Asian Americans 5 percent, Latinx 16 percent, African Americans 13 percent; the other 3 percent identify themselves as mixed race or other. It is a fact universally acknowledged more than half of all American children belong to a racial minority group. The top five countries that immigrants come from are Mexico, India, the Philippines, China and Vietnam. Despite this diversity in population, the Congress consists of more than 80 percent White and male and only about 7 percent are women of colour. In 115th Congress only 9.4 percents of its members were African American, 8.5 percent Latinx, and 3.3 percent Asian Americans. As far as number of women in the congress is concerned, in the present 117th congress, women are over a quarter of all members. Counting both the House of Representatives and the Senate, 144 of 539 seats – or 27% – are held by women.

When we, the South Asians, figure it out; we tend to say as Khalid Ahmad of The Indian Express (November 28, 2020) writes, "Kamala Harris is an American growing up in a milieu where racism was the first battle she had to fight. She is sure to look at the plight of human rights in both India and Pakistan under mounting religious discrimination." We celebrate her success but we also know that hers is more an American story than an Indian one. The Indian Express (August 14, 2020), tried to put it in perspective; "The rise of Kamala Harris is as much an Indian story as it is a part of the American dream. It is life all Indians could embrace and must celebrate enthusiastically."

When Kamala Harris was San Francisco district attorney and her political ambitions were not so obvious, she showed her inclination and co-hosted Barack Obama's fund raising campaign. Obama worked then for a small law firm and taught constitution law at the University of Chicago. Obama and Kamala

Harris met first time in 2004. Obama was about to win a U.S. Senate seat and was popular. He said in a meeting about being American, "There is not a liberal America and a conservative America. There is the United States of America. There is not a Black America and a White America and Latino America and Asian America. There's the United States of America."

Kamala Harris has repeatedly said that she tries hard to follow the approach taught by her mother Dr Shyamala Gopalan Harris that the core value of America is not just to strive for success, but also to leave the country better than they found it.

It is true that she is the first Black and South Asian American child of an immigrant parent (her mother was Indian) to attain this position. Because her father is Jamaican, she is the first person of Caribbean descent to reach this height as well. Of course Americans celebrate and never forget this. But at some point, they want that she will need to become Madame Vice President without a racial qualifier. They wish her to see as American only. It will not be out of place to cite the words written in gold letters for the two who made America so proud.

For changing the American story, for showing that the forces of empathy are greater than the furies of division, for sharing a vision of healing in a grieving world, Joe Biden and Kamala Harris both are TIME's 2020 Person of the Year.

Let me also cite from joebiden.com, the first line of "Kamala's Story":

"The first Black and Indian American woman to represent California in the United States Senate, Kamala Harris grew up believing in the promise of America and fighting to make sure that promise is fulfilled for all Americans."

In the foreword of a book titled "Run to win: Lessons in leadership for women changing the world" (2021) by Stephanie

Schriock and Christina Reynolds. Kamala Harris not only underlines the need for protecting the American dream and American democracy but also their collective responsibility and a role in fighting for the nation to get equal treatment, collective purpose and justice for all.

American Aspirations and Dreams

Kamala Harris wanted that American dream should be fulfilled and everyone should continue dreaming for it. She writes in her memoir, "The American people have not given up on the American Dream. ... But when you can't sleep at night, how can you dream?" This is a way to give the people assurance. A leader is one who assures and ensures his followers that she would leave no stone unturned to realize their dreams. The birth of her campaign slogan "for the people" is also for the same purpose.

Kamala Harris's first speech as the vice president of the US struck a chord in the hearts of American people. Her Inauguration Day address her opening remarks were, "It demonstrates who we are, even in dark times. We not only dream, we do. We not only see what has been, we see what can be. We shoot for the moon, and then we plant our flag on it. We are bold, fearless, and ambitious. We are undaunted in our belief that we shall overcome, that we will rise up."

She continued, "This is American aspiration. In the middle of the Civil War, Abraham Lincoln saw a better future and built it with land-grant colleges and the transcontinental railroad. In the middle of the civil rights movement, Dr King fought for racial justice and economic justice." As an American Kamala Harris share three outstanding values. These are: Hard work, Honesty and Decency. In fact, her words along with the president's are a symbol of the aspirational America.

"The courage to see beyond crisis, to do what is hard, to do what is good, to unite, to believe in ourselves, believe in

our country, believe in what we can do together…" This is American aspiration."

Read "Our America" (Kamala Harris, January 29, 2019). It was her launch speech in Oakland, California. "My whole life, I've only had one client: the people."

"Who are we? Who are we as Americans? So, let's answer that question… To the world… And each other…Right here… And, right now….America, we are better than this."

Mary Kay Henry, head of Service Employee International Union concludes that Kamala's whole life's work has been fighting to ensure America as a place where freedom is for everyone regardless of gender, income, or race.

There are people who will say, she isn't Black enough. There are people who will say she's not Indian enough. But one thing is certain, she is American enough.

Faith, Interfaith and so-on

As Indians, we are very curious to know about a person's caste and religion. "Kamala Harris is a Hindu Brahmin" kind of statement may please some and create animosity among others. Kamala Harris is not an Indian. She is no longer a Hindu. Her Baptist upbringing comes in the fore when she includes this quote in her speeches: "We walk by faith and not by sight." This is a quote from the New Testament's Second Letter to the Corinthians. The freedom of religious minorities is a burning issue in America also. To understand her faith let us read the following extract from her autobiography.

"My faith journey started when I was a little girl. On Sundays, my mother would dress my sister, Maya, and me in our Sunday best and send us off to the 23rd Avenue Church of God in Oakland, California, where Maya and I sang in the children's choir. That's where I formed some of my earliest

memories of the Bible's teachings. It's where I learned that "faith" is a verb, and that we must live it, and show it, in action."

"My mother, an immigrant from India, instilled the same idea in me on trips to Hindu temples. And I've also seen it reflected in the Jewish traditions and celebrations I now share with my husband, Doug. From all of these traditions and teachings, I've learned that faith is not only something we express in church and prayerful reflection, but also in the way we live our lives, do our work and pursue our respective callings."

She identifies as a Baptist — a major Protestant Christian denomination — and she was sworn in on the Bible. Though she identifies as a Baptist, she has interfaith roots. Her husband is Jewish, her father a Christian and her mother was Hindu. Religion News Service of America (Yonat Shimron, August 12, 2020) has rightly said that she is more than her gender and race. She is also the future of American religion. Nikki Haley, Bobby Jindal and several others are examples of multiple religious belonging. It is a part of America's dynamic religious landscape. One can say that her religious biography is the future of the US.

Her idea of God, a loving God, is based on the Bible: a loving God who asked us to "speak up for those who cannot speak for themselves and to defend the rights of the poor and needy."

Welcome to the club America!

Shashi Tharoor, diplomat, scholar and now a politician, welcomed Kamala Harris's victory. He reminded admiring Indians that such a moment may not have been easy to imagine in the US where there has been only one female Presidential candidate from a major political party and two vice-presidential ones-ever and all unsuccessful. But in South Asia, the glass ceiling was shattered long ago.

I must appreciate Shashi Tharoor who reminded us that just after the teenage Shyamala Gopalan arrived in the US, Srimavo Bandaranaike became the Prime Minister of Sri Lanka in 1960. And our own Indira Gandhi in 1966! The list is everlasting. Women heads of state or government currently serve in Bangladesh, Estonia, Ethiopia, and Greece. This is also noteworthy fact that Indian-origin politicians have been elected as heads of the state in various parts of the world in the last several decades, from Mauritius to Fiji. Kamala Harris as the vice president of the US will also get a pride of place in the galaxy of such stalwarts.

In response to comedian and late night host Stephen Colbert's question on Kamala Harris becoming the first female Vice President of the United States, this is what Priyanka Chopra said: "Couple of things… it was such an emotional moment for a lot of my friends and family but coming from a country like India which has seen several women in governance, whether it is President, Prime Minister…You know, welcome to the club, America. That's what I'll say. High time, I hope this isn't the first." A *Netflix* movie on Kamala's life and Kamala's role played by Priyanka isn't a bad idea! I am ready with the screen-play. Is there any taker?

And let me tell my Indian intellectuals that we in India should also acknowledge that had she remained in India, she may not have made it to the Indian vice-presidency. No woman has. There is a limit for everything, my dear argumentative Indian!

Limited but limitless: The VP Advantage

In the US there is a lot of attention on her as for them she is the first Black, South Asian, graduate of a historically Black university and an active performer in various walks of political, social and cultural life. They expect her to be Joe Biden's active partner in all things. But the constitution of the US in its Article

II says, "the vice president shall have no vote, unless (the senators) be equally divided." The Senate's own website calls the job of a VP "the least understood, most ridiculed, and most often ignored constitutional office in the federal government." Franklin Roosevelt's first vice president, John Nance Garner, once said that the title wasn't worth "a bucket of warm spit".

"I am nothing, but I may be everything." John Adams, the first Vice President, wrote of his office. He wrote to his wife, Abigail, and called the vice presidency "the most insignificant office that ever the invention of man contrived or his imagination conceived." Thomas R. Marshall, Woodrow Wilson's VP, likened the Vice President to "a man in a cataleptic fit: He cannot speak; he cannot move; he suffers no pain; he is perfectly conscious of all that goes on, but has no part in it."

But as I perceive history- maker Kamala Harris will wield real power as Vice-President. President Biden himself said that she will be the "last person in the room." It means she will be heard while making important decisions. In other words, she will be his "full partner". It is also being understood that Biden administration will follow the example of the Obama administration.

On the other hand Kamala Harris keeps in mind what Senator-turned-Vice-President Walter Mondale once pointed out, the vice presidency is the only office in our government that belongs to both executive branch and the legislative branch. She knows her responsibility that is made greater with an equal number of Democrats and Republicans in the Senate. She wrote:

"Since our nation's founding, only 268 tie-breaking votes have been cast by a Vice President. I intend to work tirelessly as your Vice President, including, if necessary, fulfilling this Constitutional duty. At the same time, it is my hope that rather than come to the point of a tie, the Senate will instead find

common ground and do the work of the American people. (San Francisco Chronicle, January 16, 2021)"

One can see that the president is treating her as an equal stakeholder. Once upon a time she was a fierce and vocal opponent of him. Now that it is the part of history and largely forgotten, He has started using inclusive "WE" instead of exclusive "I". He doesn't want any frustration to be felt.

The Vice President has already made her presence felt. For instance, she cast a tie-breaking vote in the Senate, clearing the way for Biden's $1.9 trillion corona virus stimulus package to move forward without Republican support.

During a press conference Biden was asked if he would run for re-election, he said, "Watch me… watch me." It is far from unusual for a Vice-President to harbour presidential ambitions. Other people say what they wish; I would like to say this much only, "Watch her, watch her". "Ambition" seems to be her middle name.

Can we also use the phrase "heartbeat away from the presidency" which refers to the fact that the vice president will automatically succeed the presidency in the case of the president's death, disability or resignation? After all, over the course of US history, a total of nine vice presidents have succeeded presidents in the middle of their terms. It means that there is 20% chance for her to be.

Black Women's Leadership

I have a feeling that the US was not founded with Black people in mind. Malcolm X said, "The most disrespected, unprotected, neglected person in America is the Black woman." Kamala Harris is a woman. She is a Black woman. The Black women in America are overjoyed. They are happy, not because they face hardships more than men. They are happy to see Kamala marching ahead. Kamala is a Black woman who is a source of inspiration for them. Never before had a Black person, a person of South Asian descent, or a woman held the position in American history. Her election victory was more than mere symbolism. It gave a new direction to the US. Now the Black women can turn to her for guidance. Black women have led many of the movements that have fuelled true democracy in America. But her success is remarkable among all of them. Over a century ago, it was said that Sojourner Truth asked "Ain't I a Woman?" What we do know for sure is: In 2020, her VP win is a win for *all* women, not just women of colour.

The beginning has been made. The American story that began on India's shores reached where nobody could before. She came, she saw, and she conquered. We are eager to see that day when Kamala Harris will be the President of the US. That day will see this book's second revised edition. Let me end this chapter with the words of a Nobel Prize winner poet who is a naturalized American citizen. His name is T.S. Eliot (1888-1965).

What we call the beginning is often the end.

And to make an end is to make a beginning.

The end is where we start from.

Appendix

Kamala Devi Harris has already travelled in this world for nearly 57 years. She was born in 1964. Therefore, I thought it pertinent to present for you her complete itinerary in 57 points. This will give you a cursory look at her life so far. Her life has always remained in the political limelight.

(Sources: Los Angeles Times, San Francisco Chronicle, Politico, The New Yorker, The Atlantic, NPR, USA Today, The Washington Post, The New York Times, GovTrack, The Guardian, Vox, People Magazine, The Intercept, Smart Voter, Book Riot, SF Gate, Mercury News, The Cut, The Truths We Hold by Kamala Harris.)

1. Kamala Devi Harris was born in Oakland, California on October 20, 1964, the eldest of two children born to Shyamala Gopalan, a cancer researcher from India, and Donald Harris, an economist from Jamaica.

2. Her parents met at UC Berkeley while pursuing graduate degrees, and bonded over a shared passion for the civil rights movement, which was active on campus. After she was born, they took young Kamala along to protests in a stroller.

3. Her mother chose Kamala's name from her Indian traditional heritage—Kamal means "lotus" and "Kamala" is another name for the Hindu goddess Lakshami—and the empowerment of women. "A culture that worships goddesses produces strong women," Gopalan told the Los Angeles Times in 2004.
4. Her parents divorced when she was 7, and her mother raised her and her sister, Maya, on the top floor of a yellow duplex in Berkeley.
5. In first grade, Kamala was bussed to Thousand Oaks Elementary School, which was in its second year of integration. For the next three years, she'd play "Miss Mary Mack" and cat's cradle with her friends on the bus that travelled from her predominantly black, lower-middle-class neighbourhood to her school located in a prosperous white district.
6. As a child, she went to both a Black Baptist church and a Hindu temple—embracing both her South Asian and Black identities. "My mother understood very well that she was raising two black daughters," She later wrote in her autobiography, "and she was determined to make sure we would grow into confident, proud black women."
7. She visited India as a child and was greatly influenced by her grandfather, a high-ranking government official who, it is claimed, fought for Indian independence, and grandmother, an activist who tried her level best to educate women about birth control.
8. She attended middle school and high school in Montreal after her mother got a teaching job at McGill University and a position as a cancer researcher at Jewish General Hospital.

9. In Montreal, a 12-year-old Kamala and her younger sister, Maya, led a successful demonstration in front of their apartment building in protest of a policy that banned children from playing on the lawn.

10. After high school, she attended Howard University, the prestigious historically Black college in Washington, D.C. Her subjects were political science and economics, and she joined the Alpha Kappa Alpha sorority. While attending law school in San Francisco, her sister, Maya also lived with her and she helped her in looking after Maya's daughter.

11. In 1990, after passing the bar, Harris joined the Alameda County prosecutor's office in Oakland as an assistant district attorney focusing on sex crimes.

12. Kamala's mother was initially unconvinced of her career choice. While she herself acknowledged that prosecutors have historically earned a bad reputation, she wanted to change the system from the inside.

13. In 1994, she began dating Willie Brown who was then the speaker of the state assembly and was 30 years older than her. Although Brown was legally married at the time, he had reportedly been estranged from his wife, Blanche Brown, since 1981, according to People magazine.

14. In 1995, Brown was elected mayor of San Francisco. She broke up with Brown because "she concluded there was no permanency in our relationship,"

15. After being recruited to the San Francisco District Attorney's office by a former colleague in Alameda, Harris cracked down on teenage prostitution in the city, reorientering law enforcement's approach to focus on the girls as victims rather than as criminals selling sex.

16. She reframes her prosecutorial role: "My whole life, I've only had one client: the people." GovTrack, an independent nonpartisan website, lists her as the most liberal of all 100 senators. The New York Times labels her a pragmatic moderate; Fox News hosts call her a radical.

17. In 2003, she ran for district attorney in San Francisco against incumbent Terence Hallinan, her former boss.

18. She was elected in a runoff with 56.5 per cent of the vote. With her victory, she became the first Black woman in California to be elected district attorney.

19. That same election, Gavin Newsom was elected mayor, succeeding Willie Brown.

20. During her first three years as district attorney, San Francisco's conviction rate jumped from 52 to 67 per cent.

21. One of her most controversial decisions came in 2004 when she declined to pursue the death penalty against the man who murdered San Francisco police officer Isaac Espinoza.

22. As California attorney general, Harris declined to support two ballot initiatives that would've banned the death penalty.

23. She was under scrutiny during her tenure as San Francisco district attorney when a technician stole cocaine from the DA's crime lab and mishandled evidence.

24. Her friendship with Barack Obama dates back to his run for Senate in 2004. She was first to endorse him during his 2008 presidential bid.

25. In San Francisco, she vocally supported a 2010 law that made truancy a misdemeanour and punished parents

who failed to send their children to school. The truancy rate ultimately dropped.

26. That same year, in her second term as district attorney, she ran for California attorney general.

27. The race was so tense that on election night, Cooley made a victory speech and the San Francisco Chronicle declared him the winner.

28. Three weeks later, all ballots having been counted, Harris was declared the Victor by 0.8 percentage points.

29. As attorney general, when California was offered $4 billion in a national mortgage settlement over the foreclosure crisis, she fought for a larger amount by refusing to sign the deal.

30. As attorney general, she created Open Justice system. It was an online platform to make criminal justice data available to the public. The database helped improve police accountability by collecting information on the number of deaths and injuries of those in police custody.

31. The California Department of Justice recommended in 2012 that she should file a civil enforcement action against One West Bank for "widespread misconduct" when foreclosing homes. She, however, declined to prosecute the bank or its then-CEO Steven Mnuchin.

32. She didn't support a 2015 bill in the state assembly that would have required the attorney general to appoint a special prosecutor who specializes in police use of deadly force.

33. In 2013, President Barack Obama was recorded referring to her as the "best looking attorney general in the country" He later apologized after critics labelled the comment as sexist.

34. She was said to be a potential Supreme Court nominee under the Obama administration, although she later said she wasn't interested.
35. She married Doug Emhoff, a corporate lawyer in Los Angeles, in 2014 at a small and private ceremony officiated by her sister. Emhoff has two children from his previous marriage; they call Kamala Harris "Momala."
36. She won her U.S. Senate race in 2016, defeating fellow Democrat Loretta Sanchez, a moderate congresswoman with 20 years of experience.
37. She became very famous for her sharp questioning of then-Attorney General Jeff Sessions on the Russia investigation. After 3½ minutes of persistent questioning, Sessions said, "I'm not able to be rushed this fast! It makes me nervous."
38. She implemented a similar strategy of questioning during Brett Kavanaugh's hearings in 2018. When she grilled him about whether he'd discussed the Mueller investigation with anyone, he was not able to say anything.
39. Her most fervent online supporters were called the "KHive," a phrase inspired by Beyoncé's loyal group of fans, the "Beyhive."
40. during her presidential campaign came in the first Democratic debate, when she confronted Joe Biden over his position on cross-district bussing in the 1970s while using a personal anecdote.
41. In two TV interviews over the course of a week in 2019, President Donald Trump called Harris "nasty" for her questioning of Attorney General William Barr over his handling of the Mueller report during a Senate Judiciary Committee hearing.

42. She supported the abolition of private health care during an earlier town hall. She released a health care plan that included private health insurance.
43. During the campaign, she shied away from discussing specifics about her career as a prosecutor.
44. She ended her presidential campaign in December 2019.
45. She delayed her endorsement for Biden until March 8, when there were no more women left in the race and his nomination was undeniable. Six days after the California primary, she threw her support behind Biden and said he was a leader who could "Unify the people".
46. She's a great cook who bookmarks recipes from the New York Times' cooking section and has tried almost all the recipes from Alice Waters' The Art of Simple Food.
47. She collects Converse Chuck Taylor sneakers, which are her go to travel shoes. "I love my Chucks … you know, I think it's maybe people don't expect it, but also it's a statement about who we really are. Everybody has their inner kind of Chuck look. I also think it has to do with the fact we all wanna go back to some basic stuff about who we are as a country. Chucks—whatever your background is, whatever language your grandmother spoke—you know, and we all at some point or another had our Chucks."
48. Some of her favourite books are Native Son by Richard Wright, The Kite Runner by Khaled Hosseini, The Joy Luck Club by Amy Tan, Song of Solomon by Toni Morrison, and The Lion, the Witch and the Wardrobe by C.S. Lewis.
49. She generally wakes up around 6 a.m. and works out for half an hour on the elliptical or SoulCycle. She'll start

the day with a bowl of Raisin Bran with almond milk and tea with honey and lemon before leaving for work.

50. She describes herself as a "tough" boss—although mostly on herself. "Kamala, as you all know is smart, She's tough. She's experienced. She's a proven fighter for the backbone of the country, the middle class, for all those who are struggling to get into the middle class, for all those who are struggling to get into the middle class. Kamala knows how to govern," Biden said.

51. Her father criticized her for connecting Jamaicans to the "fraudulent stereotype of a pot-smoking joy seeker." He said he and his immediate family wished "to categorically dissociate ourselves from this travesty."

52. She's not a fan of being called the "female Obama." When a reporter asked her about carrying on Obama's legacy during her run for president, she said "I have my own legacy."

53. The senator formed a close relationship with Biden's late son, Beau, when he served as the Delaware attorney general while Harris was attorney general of California. In her 2019 memoir, Harris called Beau Biden, who died of brain cancer in 2015, an "incredible friend and colleague," and wrote that she sometimes spoke with the younger Biden as many as multiple times a day in difficult moments.

54. Her motto comes from her mother: "You may be the first, but make sure you're not the last." Her inspiring line is what years ago Robert Kennedy said, "Only those who dare to fail greatly can ever achieve greatly."

55. She is the first woman, first African American and first Asian American vice president in the history of the United

States. "Leaving the door more open that was when you walked in." is her desire before saying goodbye.

56. Let me summarize her work in a nutshell. Kamala D. Harris (1964-) is a lifelong public safety and civil rights leader, and is currently serving as the Vice President of the Untied States of America. Just before that she was a U.S. Senator from California. She began her career in the Alameda County District Attorney's Office, and then was elected District Attorney of San Francisco. As California's Attorney General; Kamala prosecuted transnational gangs, big banks, Big Oil, for-profit colleges and fought against attacks on the Affordable Care Act. She also fought to reduce elementary school truancy and pioneered the nation's first open data initiated to expose racial disparities in the criminal justice system and implemented implicit bias training for police officers. The second black woman ever elected to the U.S. Senate, Kamala has worked to reform US criminal justice system, raise the minimum wage, make higher education tuition-free for the majority of Americans, and protect the legal rights of refugees and immigrants.

◻

References

'Attorney General Kamala Harris honoured for rape kit processing', CBS Sacramento, 8 April 2014.

'Full text of US Vice President-elect Kamala Harris' victory speech', Indian Express, 8 November 2020.

'Full text of US Vice President Kamala Harris' inaugural speech" YouTube.

'Kamala Harris had an affair with a 6—year-old married man when she was 29 who "launched her career"', Free Press Journal, 13 August 2020.

"Look Forward to Working Closely": PM Congratulates Joe Biden', NDTV, 8 November 2020.

Adam Edelman, "The first "second gentleman"? Meet Kamala Harris' husband, Doug Emhoff, NBC News, 13 August 2020.

Alexei Koseff, "Kamala Harris aide resigns after harassment, retaliation settlement surfaces', Sacramento Bee, 5 December 2018.

Barbara Parker and Rebecca Kaplan, "Kamala Harris's foreclosure deal a win for state', SFGate, 5 March 2012.

Ben Terris, 'Who is Kamal Harris, really? Ask her sister Maya', Washington Post 23 July 2019.

Berkeley Lovelace Jr, 'Where Kamala Harris stands on corona virus Masks, stimulus checks and other pandemic spending', CNBC, 12 August 2020.

Catherin, Kim; Stanton, Zack. "55 Things You Need to Know about Kamala Harris". Politico. August 11, 2020.

Coolbert I. King, "Kamala Harris's HBCU experience prepares her to take on Trump', Washington Post, 13 August 2020.

Dan Morain, '2 more brown associates get well-paid posts: Government: The speaker appoints his frequent companion and a long-time friend to state board as his hold on his own powerful position wanes', LA Times, 29 November 1994.

Dan Morain, Kamala's Way: An American life. Simon & Schuster.2021.

Danielle Zoellner, "Maya Harris: Who is Kamala's younger sister and why do people call her the next "Bobby Kennedy"', Independent, 13 August 2020.

David Martosko, "Half my family's from Jamaica. Are you kidding me?" Stanford professor Donald Harris, her proud Jamaican father, was not pleased. He wrote in his blog that his deceased grandmothers and parents 'must be turning in their graves," Daily Mail, 20 February 2019.

Donald Harris, "Reflections of a Jamaican Father', Jamaica Global, 18 August 2020.

Eric Lach, "Kamala Harris at the Democratic debate: "I would like to speak on the issue of race"', New Yorker, 27 June 2019.

Eugene Scott, 'Kamal Harris's post-debate discussion on Tulsi Gabbard's polling reveals something about her candidacy', Washington Post, I August 2019.

Hadley Freeman, 'More than a second gentleman: Why Doug Emhoff is Kamala Harris' secret weapon', Guardian, 21 November 2020.

Hansa Makhijani Jain, "Kamala Harris: The American Story that Began on India's Shores". Hachette India. 2021.

Heather E. Schwartz, "Kamala Harris: Madam Vice President" lerner publishing group. 2021.

Holly Honderich and Samathi Dissanayake, 'Kamala Harris: The many identities of the first woman vice-president', BBC News, 8 November 2020.

In Memoriam: Dr. Shyamala G. Harris". Breast Cancer Action. June 21, 2009.

Isabella Grullon Paz, 'Kamala Harris and Joe Biden clash on race and bussing', New York Times, 27 June 2019.

Jeffrey Gettleman, Suhasini Raj." How Kamala Harris's family in India Helped Shape Her Values". The New York Times. August 16, 2020.

Jonathan Martin, Alstead W. Herndon and Alexander Burns, "How Kamala Harris's campaign unravelled', New York Times, 30 November 2019.

Kamala Harris, 'Sen. Kamala Harris on being "Momala", Elle, 10 May 2019.

Kamala Harris, Smart on Crime: A career Prosecutor's Plan to Make Us Safer, Chronicle Books, 2009.

Kamala Harris, The Truths We Hold: An American Journey, Random House, 2019.

Kamala Harris, "Superheroes are everywhere," Penguin Random House Children's UK. 2021.

Kat Stafford, 'Kamala Harris' selection as VP resonates with Black women', Washington Post, 11 August 2020.

Katie Mettler, "As a prosecutor, Kamala Harris's doggedness was praised. As a senator, she's deemed "hysterical", Washington Post, 14 June 2017.

Kelsey Jopp, "Kamala Harris", North Star Editions. 2020.

Ken Thomas, "You Say 'Ka-MILLA', I say 'KUH-ma-la' Both Are Wrong." The Wall Street Journal.1. February 15, 2013.

Kate Woodsome, "Opinion/ You don't need to like Kamala Harris. But you should say her name properly." The Washington Post. Jan 22, 2021. Via Youtube.

Kevin Sullivan, "I am who I am": Kamala Harris, daughter of Indian and Jamaican immigrants, defines herself simply as "American", Washington Post, February 2, 2019.

Kirsten Anderson, "Who is Kamala Harris?" Penguin Workshop. 2021.

Kristen Susienka, "Kamala Harris" The Rosen Publishing Group.2020.

Lara Bazelon, 'Kamala Harris was not a "progressive prosecutor" ', New York Times, 17 January 2019.

Lisa Bonos, 'Kamala Harris's marriage inspires so many of us still searching for our Dougs', Washington Post, 9 November 2020.

Lisa Bonos, "The story of Kamala and Doug, a match made in Hollywood (literally)', Washington Post, 19 August 2020.

Manuel Roing-Forina, 'Doug Emhoff paused his career for his wife Kamal Harris's aspirations- and became the campaign's " secret weapon'", Washington Post, 27 October 2020.

Marilla Steuter-Martin, "High school friends of Kamal Harris in Montreal applaud her victory', CBC News, 7 November 2020.

Matt Bradley and Bill O'Reilly, "How Sen. Kamala Harris's Indian heritage and pioneering mother propelled her', NBC News, 20 August 2020.

Matt Viser, 'Joe Biden picks Kamala Harris as vice president', Washington Post, 11 August 2020.

Meagan Flynn, "you own them an apology": Gabbard's attack highlights Harris's complex death penalty records', Washington Post, I August 2019.

Meena Harris, "Kamala and Maya's Big Idea". Balzer+ Bray. 2020.

Michael Martinez, "A female Obama" seeks California attorney general post.CNN. October 23, 2010.

Nadia E. Brown, Danielle Casarez Lemi, "Sister Style: The Politics of Appearance for Black Women Political Elites". Oxford University Press. 2021.

Nick Bryant, "When America Stopped Being Great". Bloomsbury publishing. 2021.

Nikki Grimes, "Kamala Harris: Rotted in Justice. Atheneum Books for Young Readers. 2020.

Peter Baker and Maggie Haberman, " Trump, in interview, calls wall talks "waste of time" and dismisses investigations', New York Times, 31 January 2019.

Peter Black, "Kamala Harris's Montreal experience". Press- Republican. August 29, 2020.

Peter Byrne, "Kamala's Karma". SK Weekly. September 24, 2003.

Phil Willon, "Kamala Harris breaks a colour barrier with her US Senate win", LA Times, 8 November 2016.

Philip Elliott, "How Joe Biden enduring grief for his son helped lead him to Kamala Harris", Time, 12 August 2020.

Scott Dworkin, "Meet the Candidates 2020: Kamala Harris: A voter's guide. Skyhorse publishing.2019.

Shobha Warrier, "My niece, the US Senator", Rediff.com, 11 November 2016.

Stephanie Schriock, Christina Reynolds, "Run to Win: Lesson in Leadership for Women Changing the World. Penguin Publishing Group. 2021.

❏❏❏

Printed in the USA
CPSIA information can be obtained
at www.ICGtesting.com
LVHW051146131124
796388LV00010B/351